Managing
Interpersonal
Conflict

INTERPERSONAL COMMTEXTS

Series Editors: Mark L. Knapp & John A. Daly,
both at the University of Texas

Designed for college and university undergraduates, the **Interpersonal Commtexts** series will also interest a much larger general audience. Ideal as basic or supplementary texts, these volumes are suited for courses in the development and practice of interpersonal skills; verbal and nonverbal behavior (the basis of interpersonal transactions); functions of communication in face-to-face interaction; the development of interpersonal behavior at various points in the lifespan; and intergroup and intercultural aspects of interpersonal communication. Readable and comprehensive, the **Interpersonal Commtexts** describe contexts within which interpersonal communication takes place and provide ways to study and understand the interpersonal communication process.

Managing
Interpersonal
Conflict

William A. Donohue
with Robert Kolt

SAGE Publications
International Educational and Professional Publisher
Newbury Park   London   New Delhi

For information address:

SAGE Publications, Inc.
2455 Teller Road
Newbury Park, California 91320
E-mail: order@sagepub.com

SAGE Publications Ltd.
6 Bonhill Street
London EC2A 4PU
United Kingdom

SAGE Publications India Pvt. Ltd.
M-32 Market
Greater Kailash I
New Delhi 110 048 India

Printed in the United States of America

Library of Congress Cataloging-in-Publication Data

Donohue, William A., 1947-
  Managing interpersonal conflict / by William A. Donohue with Robert Kolt.
    p. cm. —(Interpersonal commtexts ; 4)
  Includes bibliographical references and index.
  ISBN 0-8039-3311-8 (cl). —ISBN 0-8039-3312-6 (pb)
  1. Interpersonal conflict. 2. Negotiation. 3. Conflict management. I. Kolt, Robert. II. Title. III. Series.
BF637.I48D66 1992
  303.6'9—dc20   92-11350

97 98 99 00 01 10 9 8 7 6 5

Sage Production Editor: Astrid Virding

To the two Sue's,
For their continued love and understanding

Contents

Understanding the Conflict Episode

❑ Understanding Your Own Conflict Perspective

Last week, a student described a conflict with her parents. She revealed that her parents told her and her three younger sisters that they were getting a divorce. This announcement deeply upset the student and her sisters. How could they do that to us? "I didn't even think there were any problems at home. My parents never fought," she said. "My friend's parents fought all the time before they ended their marriage. I just don't understand it." The student is still trying to adjust to the divorce. One of her sisters blames Mom for not being able to "keep" Dad. The other sisters side with their mother because they discovered that Dad dumped Mom for another woman.

This family will experience difficulty adjusting to divorce. Relationships take time to mend. Nevertheless, the couple should try to benefit from the experience after taking time to mourn the dissolved marriage. What did the breakup teach us about ourselves and our communication habits? Was it good that Mom and Dad never fought? Is that a sign of a healthy relationship? Should the family examine its own communication habits to find ways of avoiding such destructive problems?

This book expresses the importance of growing personally from conflict. Most find this concept difficult to understand. Conflict seems more like a threat than a catalyst to growth. Examine your own personal values about conflict. How do you personally react to conflict? Do you see it as a necessary part of life that brings about personal change? Maybe you see conflict as an evil part of everyone's dark side, something that people should avoid at all costs. Perhaps your family never fought so you think fighting is inappropriate.

Conflict is a part of everyone's life.

Whatever your personal perspective about conflict, one observation seems clear: Conflict is a part of everyone's life. Ask friends about their most recent conflicts. You will probably hear a very long and involved story about some incident that affected them very deeply. Many tell stories about parents getting divorced, roommates fighting over living conditions, or relational problems with significant others. These stories, and the conflicts surrounding them, often open up an individual's intimate side. They expose important values, feelings, and perspectives on the world.

This book aims to help you better understand and ultimately manage the personal conflicts you experience with others on a routine basis. What are your values concerning conflict? When is conflict appropriate? Do you get emotional when attacked and then feel compelled to attack back? Do you try to avoid conflict at all costs because it frightens you? Can you recognize when communication patterns develop in either productive or unproductive directions?

To give you a quick answer to some of these questions, complete the brief questionnaire in Table 1.1. It will help you understand your own basic conflict management preferences.

As we move through this book you will learn more about your conflict management preferences. I hope you learn to confront your own tendencies and change them, if necessary. So you can

Table 1.1 Assessing Your Reaction to Conflict

The purpose of this questionnaire is to help you assess your reaction to conflict. Respond to each statement by indicating the degree to which the statement is true for you.

If you "Never" react in the described manner, answer 1;

if you "Almost Never" react in the described manner, answer 2;

if you "Sometimes" react in the described manner, answer 3;

if you "Almost Always" react in the described manner, answer 4;

if you "Always" react in the described manner, answer 5.

When faced with a conflict, I

_____ confront it.

_____ initiate communication.

_____ think about ways to solve the problem.

_____ try to see the other side's point of view.

_____ develop a specific strategy to solve the conflict.

To find your scores, add the numbers you wrote next to each of the items. Scores range from 5 to 25. The higher your score, the more prepared you are to react positively to conflict.

view this book as a guide for handling conflicts more productively. Quite simply, if you know your strengths and limitations in conflict, like in any endeavor, your ability to manage it productively increases dramatically.

One other point about this book. The symbol on the cover represents the Chinese word for *crisis*. The top component of the symbol stands for "danger," and the bottom part stands for "opportunity." Most people recognize the danger part in conflict, but how many of us can see the opportunities in conflict? Who can see that conflict promotes the relational changes that bind people more closely together? Can anyone see the personal growth and insight that derives from an intense argument with a loved one? The opportunities in conflict are often difficult to recognize. As a result, most people choose to avoid rather than confront conflict.

In fact, Sillars, Coletti, Parry, and Rogers (1982) report that students try to *avoid* about 56% of their conflicts. They become very skilled at turning away from conflict. The opportunities they see for growth and change do not outweigh the potential dangers for them.

Although this book will present the "danger" side of conflict, it will certainly not neglect the view that conflict can promote productive change. This theme will emerge over and over again. We need to realize that conflict is a fundamental part of human life. But more important, we can use it to build better lives *if we know how to manage it*. If we fail to understand or recognize a resource of any kind, opportunity slips away.

This chapter seeks to define conflict and expose different types of conflicts. What happens when people fight, and what happens when they fail to control their fighting? This chapter now addresses these important issues.

❑ Defining Conflict

We will define conflict as a situation in which *interdependent people express (manifest or latent) differences in satisfying their individual needs and interests, and they experience interference from each other in accomplishing these goals.* Consider the various parts of this definition.

INTERDEPENDENCE

The moment that people enter conflict, or have the potential for conflict, they assume the ability to affect one another's thoughts and/or behaviors. In other words, conflict requires interdependence, and more important, it often promotes interdependence as people continue to fight. For example, have you ever experienced a situation in which you became closer to someone after an argument? You cleared the air, you got emotional, and suddenly you found the relationship had reached a new plateau. When conflict occurs among people, each sends the message, "I can't get what I want without going through you." So in a very real sense, the more people enter conflict, the more they admit they depend on each other. After the conflict, people may decide to terminate the relationship, thereby ending the interdependence. But when conflict continues, people reaffirm their interdependence by simply confronting one another to achieve their goals. They may not like or trust one another, but they remain interdependent.

MANIFEST-LATENT

america protest society? (handwritten)

Conflict also varies according to the extent to which it is out in the open (manifest) or hidden from view (latent). Manifest conflicts present themselves to us daily. We see war, political strife, and dissent in every corner of the globe. This conflict is a sign that people have differences and they need to express them. Certainly, the heart of American democracy, the First Amendment to the Constitution that guarantees freedom of speech, lays the foundation for manifest conflict. It establishes a priority for exposing differences in a responsible, nonviolent manner so people can be aware of problems and do something about them.

In contrast, latent conflict consists of differences that remain hidden from view. As indicated above, the most common conflict management strategy is avoidance. People develop the habit of not exposing differences. Many parents raise their children to avoid conflict by telling them not to talk about certain topics. Children often see their parents act uncomfortably when discussing sensitive issues. And parents might switch the topic when children express different opinions.

journal (handwritten)

What messages about conflict did you perceive as a child in your home? In what ways did your parents either avoid conflict or communicate to you that conflict should be avoided? The student described at the beginning of this chapter discovered the dangers of overavoidance. She misread lack of conflict as a sign of a healthy relationship. What she was really saying was that her parents never expressed differences. They kept their differences hidden, resulting in latent conflict that led to the breakup of their marriage. The issue of *avoidance* will surface repeatedly in this book because it is one of the most significant conflict problems people face.

NEEDS AND INTERESTS

Needs are defined as basic human desires tied to self-concept or self-esteem. For example, you might think of yourself as a good, honest, reliable person. This self-concept makes you believe that others should treat you with respect and dignity. If they treat you with a lack of respect, it strikes at the heart of your self-esteem because you believe you deserve better treatment. Desires for respect, dignity, freedom, recognition, and self-worth are needs. You can't live without them; you need them to feel good about yourself. Interests, on the other hand, are desires that live apart from an individual's self-concept. You would like to have certain things, but you can live without them.

Perhaps the best example of the difference between the two concepts lies in occupational goals. In any occupation, most people probably want financial security and fulfillment with their work. You are probably no exception. However, if you had to choose between the two, which would you pick? Is fulfillment more important than money or vice versa? If you were poor but enjoyed your work tremendously could your self-esteem survive?

Why is this distinction important for conflict? If you begin fighting about your needs, do you think the dispute will become more or less intense than if you begin fighting about your interests? Needs-centered disputes are more likely to become intense and lead to a dead end. For example, if you challenge another person's needs, you are essentially saying to that person, "You need to change who you are."

Consider a person's need for freedom. If you deny another person's right to freedom, then you face a needs-centered conflict. The only way you can "win" the conflict is for the other person to no longer need freedom. Given that freedom is likely to be a core part of that person's self-esteem, you are thus asking the person to change their fundamental view of themselves. People are likely to defend themselves at all costs against such fundamental challenges, resulting in very intense conflict. One of the first tasks this book will ask you to is label your conflicts as needs centered or interests centered. If they are needs centered, we will discuss strategies for moving them to more interests-centered disputes so they can be constructively addressed.

The important needs listed in Table 1.2 can generate a great deal of destructive conflict if others challenge them. Reflect on your last serious conflict. Did the other party challenge any of

Table 1.2 Assessing Your Personal Needs

The purpose of this questionnaire is to assess your personal needs. Listed below are 10 personal needs. Check off the 3 most important personal needs in your life right now.

_____ Respect from my friends.

_____ Freedom to make my own decisions.

_____ My sexual identity (being a man or a woman).

_____ Respect from my professional peers.

_____ Religious freedom.

_____ Monetary wealth.

_____ Personal appearance.

_____ My identity as a parent, brother, sister, or child.

_____ To be liked by my friends.

_____ Personal safety and security.

---

your important needs? Chances are that the conflict involved some of these needs. And, if you failed ultimately to satisfy those needs, then you probably also failed to reach a satisfactory solution to the conflict.

INTERFERENCE

Finally, conflict is triggered by perceived interference. When both parties see the other as standing in the way of goal attainment, conflict flares up. However, parties feel no need for conflict if they perceive no resistance to their goals. Why rock the boat if nothing stands in its way? For example, consider the divorce situation described previously. Assume that originally the husband wanted to terminate the marriage but the wife wished to remain married. The husband wants change, but the wife is happy with the status quo. Sensing resistance, the husband initiates conflict to divorce his wife. However, the wife resists conflict because she resists change. She wants the marriage to continue. So she avoids conflict because she gains nothing by fighting.

However, as the husband perceives more resistance to change, he may initiate other problems to motivate the wife to get divorced —problems that create resistance from the wife. For example, he might try to criticize, harass, or just make life difficult for her. Resistance (and the amount of resistance) triggers manifest conflict. As the conflict matures, individuals may remove their "resistance points" and work together to resolve their differences. Nevertheless, early resistance brings the conflict out in the open.

These four elements—interdependence, manifest-latent, needs and interests, and interference—are important reference points in understanding conflict situations. They reveal where the conflict is likely to go. When people fight about needs issues like power and respect, they stimulate tremendous interference from one another and create more interdependence until the fight is over.

Consider your fights over the last several months. Have you felt insulted, put down, or in other ways offended by another person? If so, you probably defended yourself using very intense communication tactics including attacks, rude comments, and possibly threats. When others threaten our basic needs, we want to defend ourselves. This defense requires increased interdependence because we must work closely (but unpleasantly) with the other person to resolve the problem. And because such resolutions are often difficult, they consume time and emotional energy. That is, we put more into the conflict when others threaten our needs. So a snowball effect takes over. More time and more involvement mean more interdependence. We work hard, together, to resolve the problem.

This book seeks to steer you away from the kind of destructive conflict that threatens personal needs. We hope to provide you with the courage and the tools to develop constructive conflicts that explore alternative perspectives on issues. To view this goal more clearly, it is important to look at the features of constructive and destructive conflict.

❏ Constructive and Destructive Conflict

WHAT DOES CONSTRUCTIVE CONFLICT LOOK LIKE?

Perhaps you currently participate in a very personal relationship with someone. We become very close to our friends and relatives, and we develop strong intimate ties with loved ones. When we experience disputes with these individuals, can they ever be productive? Yes they can, but the key lies in seeing the difference between constructive and destructive conflict. For example, consider the situation in which two classmates are debating the merits of a university proposal to raise tuition. The dialogue goes something like this:

EDWARD: As much as it hurts me personally, I think the university should raise tuition so they can use the money to attract more minority faculty.

JANET: They could choose other ways of attracting minority faculty. The cost of education is driving away minorities from the university.

EDWARD: Yes, but the increased tuition money can be used to fund more minority scholarships.

JANET: I can't believe how ignorant you are about university politics. Can't you see that they will spend the money any way they want?

EDWARD: Who are you calling ignorant? I read more than you do.

JANET: I'm sorry. I didn't mean to say you weren't well informed. I'm just frustrated by the money situation.

Was this a constructive or destructive conflict? Were there elements of each type of conflict present in this bit of interaction? To answer these questions consider this list of criteria for a constructive conflict.

Constructive conflicts are:

1. *Interests centered.* Basic personal needs to preserve power and save face remain unthreatened.
2. *Manifest.* People discuss their differences and confront them openly.
3. *Capable of bolstering interdependence.* When people use conflict to learn more about one another's ideas and perspectives, conflict helps bind people together.
4. *Focused on flexible means for solving the dispute.* Adopting a position of flexibility in how you reach your goal communicates a willingness to work with the other party.

5. *Committed to both parties accomplishing their goals.* If both parties can commit to mutual goal attainment, they state that they care about the relationship and want it to succeed.

Now, consider this set of criteria for destructive conflicts:

1. *Needs centered.* When individuals attack one another's personal rights for freedom and dignity, they threaten the rewarding quality of relationships.
2. *Focused on personalities and not behaviors.* If you are told by someone that you have a particular personal trait problem (such as intelligence or rigidness) how do you react? People reject such labels because they imply that people are incapable of changing and becoming more cooperative.
3. *Involved in power preservation and face saving.* The goal in destructive conflicts is to save your own power and your own self-image while making the other person look bad.
4. *Aimed at compromising interdependence.* Conflicts turn potentially destructive when individuals try to destroy trust and get even with the other person. The rush for revenge tears apart the underlying bonds in a relationship.
5. *Concentrated on narrowly defined goals and short-cut problem solving.* When individuals become emotionally involved in attacking or defeating the other party, they become very focused on that one task. This focus discourages systematic problem-solving activities such as considering multiple options and active information seeking.
6. *Frequented by extended, uncontrolled escalation or avoidance cycles.* Think of a conflict cycle as a set of behaviors that repeat themselves. Destructive cycles can involve attacking and defending comments, for example. Or avoidance can become cyclical when one person expresses a problem while the other changes the topic or makes a joke. When repeated often, this pattern becomes a destructive way of handling the conflict. Such retaliation and avoidance cycles often culminate in violence.

Now take another look at Janet and Edward's dialogue. How did the dialogue start and how did it end? You probably noticed that the first three statements focused on the issues without any personal attacks. Then Janet called Edward ignorant. This personal accusation is the first sign of any potentially destructive conflict in the dialogue. Edward defends himself in his next statement and accuses Janet of not reading as much as he does. His goal turns away from the issues and toward saving face. Can you see how quickly and easily one short comment can sidetrack a productive conflict? After all, she attacked his personal need for a positive self-image. Attacking a person's needs moves interaction quickly away from problem solving.

Janet's final comment, an apology, provides an interesting conclusion to the sequence. In this comment she repairs the relational damage in an attempt to move the conflict away from personal tensions and back toward the issue of tuition increases. As we shall learn later, such relational repair is a powerful technique for stopping a needs-centered conflict cycle. It also serves as a powerful technique for improving relational strength, because it brings out into the open how people feel about one another. This is the opportunity part of conflict. This conflict gave Janet an opportunity to tell Edward that she valued the relationship and wanted to preserve and probably strengthen it. Have you ever experienced similar feelings after such a discussion?

Consider two final points about constructive and destructive conflicts. First, not all conflicts can make an easy transition from a destructive to a constructive mode. Many conflicts remain destructive because people cannot pull together the communication skills necessary for constructive problem solving. The key lies in learning the communication skills capable of turning conflict around.

Second, a conflict's constructive and destructive quality depends on time. *During* the conflict, people may see it as destructive. However, *after* the conflict, people may see it as very constructive. It helped reveal hidden issues that needed attention. Perhaps the couple lacked the ability to discuss its concerns openly. Like most people, the pair probably needed a destructive blowup to expose important differences. Of course, the opposite might also happen. A conflict that looked constructive at the time might later appear destructive, because it failed to expose hidden issues. So keep in mind the time element when exploring the constructive and destructive nature of conflict.

At this point, it might be useful to outline how conflicts escalate and to understand how they can be turned into more productive interactions.

❏ Levels of Conflict and Tension

LEVEL 1: NO CONFLICT

The first level of conflict is, of course, no conflict. Individuals face no key differences in goals. This level facilitates productive communication *as long as people feel free to express differences when they arise.* That is, people grow comfortable with "no conflict"; they don't want to rock the boat. When a problem arises, they put it off or dismiss it completely. Most communications occur without significant goal differences. So it is easy to get used to it and to protect it. However, as we know from the list of destructive conflicts, latent conflicts can boil over and become big problems. Avoiding conflict just to preserve a state of no conflict amounts to asking for trouble.

For example, a student recently expressed concern about her relationship with her long-term boyfriend. She said that they were going to get married after graduation. She just knew it would work because they never had a fight in the three years they dated. But she was a little concerned because they were starting to discuss how they were going to handle job location after graduation and marriage. She wanted him to follow her because she could command a high salary as an engineering major. She claimed he had not thought about the issue and believed they should put off the decision until after graduation.

Never having a fight should be a danger sign to this couple. It probably means they fear discussing anything controversial or, perhaps, they care little about the relationship. The lack of practice at knowing how to resolve conflicts productively will hurt them when a real challenge comes along. The graduation problem is a real challenge for this couple. The student should call the issue to her boyfriend's attention and insist on discussing it.

LEVEL 2: LATENT CONFLICT

Frequently, conflicts become an uneven business. One person senses a problem and believes goal differences exist. Yet, the other gives no sign of noticing such differences or tries to deny that differences exist. Even if people live with these differences, latent conflict is different from no-conflict situations. When conflict remains latent, at least one person feels some concern, which keeps growing in that person's mind. Perhaps he or she forgets about the problem, and it reverts to a no-conflict situation. Or the problem can become more intense and eventually build into a manifest conflict.

The student's problem with her boyfriend serves as a good example of this process. Recall that she tried to discuss the job location problem with her fiancé, but he rejected her request. She sensed goal differences, exposed them, and tried to initiate some discussion of the issue. At that point, a no-conflict situation turned into a latent-conflict situation. Her concerns will not go away and will build to the point at which she will force a discussion of the issue. If not, the issue could simply disappear from her list of concerns for a variety of reasons, and the situation could revert to a no-conflict situation.

LEVEL 3: PROBLEMS TO SOLVE

When people finally express concerns that focus on interests, they reach Level 3 conflicts. Note that at this level, their goals do not include personal attacks or saving face. They remain fairly focused on the problem. This definition does not deny that from time-to-time people slip in and out of more person-focused conflict. Janet and Edward's dialogue found them digressing into a potentially destructive conflict. Janet pulled them out with an apology, and they were able to retain their focus on the problem.

By reaching and then sustaining this level of conflict, parties improve their chances of making their conflict yield constructive outcomes. Furthermore, they give important information to each other. The first statement they make is that they are willing to take the risks needed to grow. Clearly, the parties could have remained at a latent conflict level and tried to live with the problem. But they chose to confront it and that took courage to face the risks associated with that confrontation.

Second, couples also show concern for the relationship when they finally reach this level of conflict. By keeping their discussions centered on the issues, even if the issues involve how they feel about one another, they show concern for the other person and for preserving the relationship. Again, Janet and Edward's dialogue demonstrated how parties keep focused on the issues, probably strengthening their relationship at the same time.

LEVEL 4: DISPUTE

A dispute involves a problem to solve that also carries with it a needs-centered conflict. Individuals fight about an issue but insert frequent personal attacks that move the conflict more toward a destructive orientation. When conflicts reach this level, the needs-centered dimension of the conflict takes precedence over the problem because people's first priority is self-protection, not the original substantive problem. Have you noticed in your own disputes how quickly people get off track when they turn personal? These conflicts can escalate out of control and ultimately can result in physical violence.

How do you pull back to focus on the issues? Certainly, this book is about that specific problem. If you can focus on the problem, you begin the process of constructive problem solving. When disputes stay with this process, people have the best chance of clearing the air and exposing new ideas. However, the trick in moving back to problem solving involves addressing the needs-centered issues first. People cannot talk about substance until they feel respected and dignified. Can you work with people who say they do not respect you? Few people can problem solve in this context. So the strategy involves granting the other's personal needs so they do not interfere in the discussions of substantive problems. Remember, the longer people spend in a destructive-conflict mode the less likely they are to share information and focus on the issues. Threatened people focus on protecting themselves and not on working out a problem.

LEVEL 5: HELP

When people can no longer manage their dispute because they've gotten out of control (probably with personal, needs-centered issues), they often seek help. These cries for help generally appear after many failed attempts at handling the dispute. In Chapter 7, we examine how people can receive help in handling their conflicts. People might ask for a counselor, a mediator, or even a lawyer if things get out of hand. Nevertheless, when parties reach out for help they are tacitly saying that they are tired, frustrated, and want someone else to lend a hand.

Sometimes parties reach out to friends. Friends and relatives ask those they trust to intervene in disputes. Friends should simply listen, because they take great risks getting involved in other people's disputes. Your friends will look to you to take their side. They look for support, because they feel personally attacked. "Lick my wounds," he or she cries, while telling you a tale of woe.

You may have guessed that the general strategy of those providing assistance is, first, to get the main parties talking again if the dispute has not escalated into verbal or physical abuse. People need to feel secure when communicating with others. Then, once people are talking, they need some strategy for reducing the potential for destructive conflict cycles to resurface. Various forms of third-party conflict management help achieve this goal (such as mediation), and they will be described later. Nevertheless, the goal is to use the third party initially as protection. Then the third party can help the couple come to grips with its problems.

LEVEL 6: FIGHT/FLIGHT

What happens when help fails or when parties become so angry that they don't think of asking for help? When parties reach this point, we can call it the "fight/flight" level of conflict. This label specifies a key conflict decision point for the parties. Either they move against and try to defeat (or even destroy) the other party or they try to escape from the situation. Whatever decision parties make, the objective remains the same. In general, when people reach the fight/flight point in a conflict, they send signals that indicate they want a pretty serious restructuring of the relationship. They might want to terminate the relationship because it is too painful. Or they might fight or flee to see how the other party feels about them.

Did you ever know someone who tried to break off a relationship after a big fight because he or she felt stepped on? Well, sometimes breaking up is really an attempt to get more power in the relationship. By breaking up, the party sends the message, "Hey, I don't need you to be happy." Less need means less dependency and, therefore, more power or control over the person. The point is that reaching a point of fighting or fleeing generally means a serious relational restructuring is about to be attempted.

Of course, when parties reach the fight/flight level of intensity, they grow very emotional. Emotions intensify because, by the time the conflict has reached this level, personal needs, important values, or major principles have become the exclusive focus of the conflict. The conflict moves way beyond issues that are negotiable when fight/flight impulses set in. When others threaten our personal needs for personal safety, freedom of expression, and dignity, we become defensive. We forget about negotiation. Chapter 3 explores the specific triggers of emotional reactions. But the important point remains that people use these emotions for self-protection.

In fact, in the fight/flight mode, people seek all the protection they can find. Friends, relatives, or anyone can serve this protection role. People might flee to friends or family in time of need. Or they might ask friends to help them fight. Nevertheless, protection is the key need, and people search everywhere for it.

Have you ever been on the edge of the fight/flight decision?

Have you ever been on the edge of the fight/flight decision? If so, you probably discovered that you spoke in stereotypes. You see people not as individuals but as those who belonged to some group. Why did you do this? The answer lies in the emotions. When charged up emotionally, you experience difficulty seeing shades of gray. We retreat into gross or very obvious ways of evaluating people. For example, in racial conflicts that deteriorate into rioting, all people see is color and not individual characteristics.

How can parties move back from the fight/flight level? A better way of asking this question is: How can parties begin negotiating or at least agreeing to mediate the dispute? The key to achieving this objective involves eliminating violations of personal needs. When people no longer feel fear or resistance to their sacred values and principles, they can begin to calm down and think. Unfortunately, giving an enemy respect or showing trust to a hated foe is difficult. However, moving back levels of conflict cannot be achieved without making this move first.

LEVEL 7: INTRACTABLE

Finally, we add the time element to conflict. When people remain at the fight/flight level for a long period of time, sustaining the conflict becomes more important than resolving it. That is, the conflict gains a life of its own. In the other levels of conflict, we assumed that people could retreat to a lower level sooner or later. For example, if the parties successfully achieved an agreement in mediation, they might try problem solving on their own in the future. However, when the conflict becomes intractable, people abandon hope for a constructive solution. The conflict remains in place for a long period of time, perhaps until parties destroy one another or they lose the will to continue the fight.

Negative public pronouncements about the conflict and the enemy are good signs that parties place the conflict in the intractable stage. Parties see themselves as part of a *cause*, fighting for fundamental principles that cannot be compromised in any way. The causes might include rights for reproductive freedom, as in the intractable prochoice-antiabortion conflict. Or the cause might involve religious freedom and homeland rights as in the Arab-Israeli conflict. The cause is the key. When people start talking about "the cause," the conflict has gained a life of its own.

The reason intractable conflicts gain a life of their own is that people view the cause as more important than victory. Think about that for a moment. Can you imagine a situation in which sustaining the conflict is more important than withdrawing from it? Certainly, every country that has gone to war believes in that principle. Couples who fight long after their divorce may believe that stopping the fight would be more painful than continuing it.

One interesting effect of prolonged, intractable conflict deals with leadership emergence. People look for strong leadership and rely more on their directives during periods of prolonged conflict. This reliance makes sense when focusing on emotions. As indicated above, this kind of intractable conflict stirs emotions. With emotions stirred up, a leader can step in to further stir up emotions. People are very vulnerable to messages that support their point of view, particularly if the leader speaks to the personal needs that the conflict threatens.

For example, historians often attribute Hitler's rise to power to the vulnerability of the German population after World War I. After that war, the Allies made the Germans pay large war reparations to punish them for their aggression. These payments, along with a destroyed industrial base, placed the Germans in an economic crisis and threatened their sense of German nationalism. Hitler spoke emotionally about this nationalism and secured the support of the German people. The people were vulnerable, and a leader stepped forth who spoke directly to their needs.

USING THE PHASES

Look on these conflict phases as a way of thinking about how conflict can progress, not necessarily about how conflict actually evolves every time. Some conflicts might begin immediately as disputes and move quickly to the intractable stage. Others might stabilize at the level of problems to solve. Still others might vacillate between the problem and dispute phases.

The important point is that the phase should dictate the general approach you use to deal with the conflict. For example, if several very significant relational issues arise, the disputants might find themselves in the dispute phase or even the fight/flight stage. If you ignore these relational issues and assume that the dispute lies in the problems-to-solve phase, then you might incorrectly avoid the heart of the conflict. If parties are at the fight/flight level, they will require more severe interventions.

Think of a conflict in which you recently participated. How did the conflict evolve? Was it latent for a while and then it progressed to a dispute stage? What brought it back to a problem phase, if in fact you achieved this objective? Looking at your own conflicts in light of this phase model is the first step toward constructive conflict management.

❑ Some Principles Guiding Conflict Development

For most people, conflicts pose very grave threats. Few of us want conflict or view it as an opportunity for growth. All those emotions during conflicts stimulate fear about all the consequences of change. Harnessing the energy from conflict requires understanding more about how it works and evolves over time. Phases were discussed, but why do phases emerge? Why do so many conflicts spiral out of control? This chapter now turns to these questions.

PRINCIPLE 1: CONFLICT PATTERNS
PERPETUATE THEMSELVES

Recall the point made previously that intractable conflicts frequently gain a life of their own. The reason cited for this perpetuation dealt with the idea that intractable conflicts sooner or later become a *cause* for the disputants. Fighting and violence is better than peace. But there is a more fundamental principle at work here. The principle is that conflicts feed into themselves and become cyclical. Throughout this book you will learn about various kinds of conflict cycles experienced by all kinds of people in any number of conflict situations. Once conflicts begin, they take on a cyclical form.

For example, one party makes a comment that threatens a personal need. The speaker might even utter the words very innocently intending only to make an observation or perhaps a request. Nevertheless, the hearer perceives the comment as offensive and immediately strikes back verbally. This aggressive retort brings about another retort and the cycle becomes clearly visible. Any assessment of your own arguments will probably reveal these cycles. Only when you can see the cycles will you have a chance of breaking away from them and deescalating the conflict to a more productive level.

What influences how cycles evolve? Certainly, many variables can steer conflicts in different directions. One key variable deals with role relationships. People's conflicts with their spouses evolve differently from conflicts with their bosses. The professional and personal roles people enact generally dictate how the cycles will evolve. Maybe you snap back more readily to an intimate friend than to your boss. Most people do. Because roles exert so much influence on conflict cycles, the chapters in this book will discuss cycles with respect to roles. For example, the kinds of conflict cycles married couples experience will be a big part of Chapter 3.

PRINCIPLE 2: CONFLICT IS ALWAYS
CONTEXTUAL

All conflicts occur within some social or institutional context. The point about roles influencing conflict cycles illustrates this point. People are always in some kind of role relationship, and this relationship is part of the communication context. So, understanding conflict cycles requires understanding roles.

However, other important features of the context also influence how conflict evolves. For example, in all social settings, people have traditions, habits, and rituals for handling conflict. Perhaps you come from a culture in which people intentionally start conflicts because they enjoy the action. They yell and scream at one another all the time. Or your family might go out of its way to avoid conflicts at all costs. Both of these extremes represent different rituals or habits in handling conflicts. Even when we don't know someone personally, we draw on our cultural habits for handling conflict.

The principle here is simple, but very important: *Don't overlook the context when trying to understand the conflict.* Look at communication rituals and habits as strong indicators of how the parties will handle the conflict. If parties are generally not open with one another, how well can they deal with problems when they arise? Failure to be open leaves people vulnerable for quick escalation of conflict to unproductive phases. The context provides a great deal of information about the conflict and needs your attention.

PRINCIPLE 3: CONFLICT ALWAYS HAS RELATIONAL IMPLICATIONS

No matter what the conflict is about, the parties can count on some kind of relational change when it's over. The changes might feel insignificant when parties discuss simple problems. Or the changes might seem very profound, particularly when conflict escalates into the fight/flight phase. Perhaps parties experience subtle adjustments to their power relations after conflict by feeling like they hold more rights to express themselves in the relationship. Or parties might grow closer to one another after working out their problems.

Why do relationships change more when people engage in conflict? They change more during conflict because relational issues are a part of every conflict at any phase. When people have problems to solve, the relational issues may be secondary to the substantive issues, but they are still there. For example, consider a mother-daughter conflict in which the daughter wants to start dating and the mother rejects the idea. Even if the discussion stays at a low-key problem level, the daughter's resistance shows a desire to change power relations with her mom. The daughter is proposing a new mother-daughter relationship with more equal power through which issues like dating can be discussed. Certainly, as the conflict moves more toward the intractable level, proposed changes in the relationship grow even more severe.

Watch for relational changes when conflict erupts.

The key point of this principle is simple. Watch for relational changes when conflict erupts. Parties not only need to keep track of the main problems but need to be sure that the relational restructuring is moving in the desired direction.

PRINCIPLE 4: MANIFEST CONFLICT
SERVES MANY FUNCTIONS

When people finally confront conflict they should be aware that the conflict can serve many functions beyond solving problems.

(1) Conflict Bonds Parties Together to Fight a Common Enemy. The members of a divorcing couple might hate each other one minute, but bond together very closely if someone threatens their baby whom they both love very dearly.

(2) Conflict Serves a Group-Preserving Role. Groups would often fall apart if they could not discuss and work out their differences. Group conflicts can get out of control and even destroy the group. But the opportunity to discuss differences helps the group both to work together and to cope with its challenges.

(3) Conflict Helps Define Roles. Were you ever involved in a group discussion that was going nowhere? Finally, someone expressed frustration at the lack of progress and the group members found themselves involved in conflict about the best way of doing things. This conflict pointed out the need for the group to get organized. They needed a leader and someone to take minutes. This conflict helped people see the ambiguity in the roles and the need to straighten them out to make any progress in the meeting.

(4) Conflict Increases Understanding of Feelings. When conflict intensifies, the potential for emotional expression increases. After all, personal needs get violated, people become defensive, and emotions can erupt. As a result, conflict often becomes the vehicle for people to express their emotions about a certain issue. They might be reluctant to reveal feelings in nonconflict situations, but once in the conflict, they get pushed into revealing feelings. Many people experience difficulty revealing feelings when not in conflict.

Consider a person who expressed frustration about the future of her relationship. Asked if she experienced any conflict with this other person, she said, "Well no, everything's just fine there." This couple needed the conflict to help them express emotions.

They were incapable of just sitting down and talking about their feelings about each other. Do you know any couples with similar difficulties?

(5) Conflict Not Only Helps to Clarify Feelings but Also Has the Same Effect on Issues. People may not know one another's positions on issues without some conflict to force the issues out into the open. Conflict certainly exhibits this feature in divorce mediation. Couples in mediation often discuss issues about raising children that they could not, or would not, discuss during the marriage. Because the conflict focuses on the children, they can get all the issues out on the table.

(6) Conflict Helps Preserve Minority Rights. It serves this function because the majority population often remains unaware that minority rights are being violated. Society needs conflict to point out these rights violations. The majority may feel uncomfortable with the confrontation. But if the confrontation continues to focus on the issue and not turn to a fight/flight situation, it probably increases its chances of success. Of course, some argue that in extreme rights violation situations, violence is not only necessary but morally justified. How do you feel about whether violence is ever justified?

❏ Conclusions

You can find the most important point about this chapter on the cover of this book. Again, the Chinese symbol for *crisis* points out that we must see both the dangers and opportunities inherent in conflict. Dangers emerge with the continuous violation of personal needs when no attempt is made to move away from these violations. Opportunities emerge when people stay focused on the issues and continue a vigorous dialogue about the best way to solve the problem. Whenever people complain about their conflicts, they should first think about the opportunities. Chances to clarify feelings and issues and to improve relationships come along so infrequently in life.

Unfortunately, most people fail to see the opportunities in conflict situations. Emotions blind us to these opportunities. We get excited, we believe the other person is *completely* at fault, and we try to work around them. A colleague once described this problem of not seeing the opportunities as "getting stupid." She described what happens to your brain during intense conflict: "All the energy rushes from the thinking part of your brain to the feeling part. This makes you stupid and incapable of thinking."

The concept of "getting stupid" makes sense. Have you ever felt out of control in a conflict? Words came out of your mouth that you never intended to say. Most people face this reality. You end up getting into more trouble because you couldn't think before you spoke. You got stupid. Put in these terms, the real purpose of this book is to delay your "getting stupid" in future conflicts.

It all comes down to one simple insight. If, in the middle of a conflict, you suddenly say to yourself, "Gee, I'm getting stupid," then you are on the way to opportunity. This one insight shows that you can think, because you are at that moment capable of objectively reflecting on your own behavior. That one comment is like holding a mirror in front of yourself while you are fighting. You see what you are doing. Only when you see what you are doing can you begin to correct it.

So here is the challenge before you. After reading this book, the one skill you should hope to achieve is the ability to say during a conflict, "Gee, I'm getting stupid." If you do that, then reading this book will be justified in that one moment.

2

Confronting Conflict

The last chapter ended with a challenge. Try to avoid getting stupid during conflict. Is this objective possible? Can we begin conflict without it blowing up in our faces? The first step in accomplishing this objective involves making the decision to confront or avoid the conflict. Many people might make this decision without really thinking about it. They simply go with their usual practice of either confronting or avoiding.

Consider the family that went out of its way to avoid the conflict at all costs. It's as if they had a big, stinky elephant in their living room and no one wanted to admit that it was there. The whole family walked on eggshells, afraid to say anything that might offend anyone. Most people prefer to deal with conflict by avoiding it. This family is typical in this regard. Of course, either confronting or avoiding is not necessarily always unproductive. When to confront and when to avoid conflict is the key to the problem.

The purpose of this chapter is to explore this choice, because it is the first decision parties make in addressing their conflict. The decision can be very difficult, particularly when you see the conflict moving in a destructive direction. Your natural tendency is to try to avoid the conflict as long as possible. Should you fight that impulse and jump into the dispute or should you continue to avoid the conflict?

Unfortunately, others often present us with few real choices in confronting conflict. Another person might decide to confront and engage you in conflict right away. He or she might even prevent your escape and require your participation in the fray. Hostage negotiations exemplify this forced confrontation. Police cannot choose whether or not to get involved in hostage- taking events. When someone takes hostages the police need to rush in and try to negotiate the release of those hostages. Sometimes people may engage you in a conflict and you simply have no choice but to confront the situation. However, even in these circumstances, there is some choice about delaying the conflict or dealing with it right away. When should you confront the conflict and when should you delay it?

There are three decision issues. *The first decision is whether or not to confront.* Should you risk the move to jump in or take the risk and avoid the conflict hoping for productive outcomes? If you make the decision to confront, then your next decision deals with timing. *The second decision is when to confront the conflict.* Should the confrontation be delayed, or pressed immediately? *The third decision, of course, relates to how to confront the conflict.* What is the best approach to make in dealing with this problem? This chapter deals these three issues and should provide you with some guidelines for deciding if, when, and how to confront your conflict.

❑ Decision 1: Should I Confront the Conflict?

DOES CONFRONTATION WORK?

The decision to confront conflict is certainly complex and often very personal. Is confrontation effective? It seems safe to conclude that, in general, confrontation works better than avoiding conflict. Research in organizational communication (Putnam & Wilson, 1982) tells us that employees respect managers more when they confront problems as opposed to avoid them. Employees regard managers who avoid problems as not doing their job, because they are not trying to solve organizational problems.

What about conflict in personal relationships? To answer this question we can turn to research in marital communication. We know from a variety of studies (e.g., Gottman, 1979; Noller, 1988; Sillars & Wilmot, 1989) that happily married couples confront conflict, whereas those with marital problems go out of their way to avoid it. In particular, happily married couples listen to each other's concerns and then negotiate any differences. Does confrontation *cause* the couple to be happily married? The evidence fails to support a direct cause, but the two appear related. When people can discuss their problems, and they want to continue the relationship, confronting conflict appears to be generally productive.

RELATIONAL IMPORTANCE

Consider these other factors when making the confrontation decision. For example, the importance of the relationship weighs heavily on the decision. Is the relationship worth saving or not? If it is important, then the person wants to see it grow and prosper. In general, will confronting the conflict help or hinder relational growth? The answer is that it can do both. Confrontation will help the relationship if both people value it because the confrontation tends to clarify important feelings and issues dividing parties. However, if one or both parties want to destroy the relationship, confrontation might give them that opportunity. So assess both parties' interests in preserving the relationship. If it is worth the effort, confrontation is probably the best decision.

ISSUE TYPE AND SIGNIFICANCE

A second decision point about confrontation relates to the significance and type of issues in dispute. In general, important issues are strong candidates for confrontation. After all, avoiding

an important problem may be a big roadblock to your relationship with the other person. For example, many married couples
run away from discussing important financial or child-rearing
differences. Left undiscussed, these problems always grow. Then,
parties risk the loss of trust and intimacy in their relationship.

However, not all issues require confrontation. Fighting about
every little thing is disruptive and time consuming. In fact, we
tend to regard people that confront others about every problem
as complainers. It is natural to shy away from people who complain too much. So be selective about which issues bear confrontation and pick the important ones whenever possible.

Not only is issue importance a critical deciding factor but so is
the type of issue. Take a look at the kinds of issues married couples
fight about. Couples with unhappy marriages fight more about
relational problems, including trust, power, and intimacy. Their
difficulty lies in failing to stick with the fight long enough to develop
options for addressing the relational concerns. In contrast, couples who are more happily married stay with these concerns and
eventually work them out. Once past these relational problems,
they can concentrate on dealing with differences over their substantive interests or factual matters of some kind. The lesson here
is that relational problems should be addressed as soon as they
arise because these issues threaten personal needs. Remember,
when we threaten personal needs, progress on other issues comes
to a halt.

What about value conflicts? Should individuals also confront
them with the same high priority as relational conflicts? When
people disagree over values, they stand a small chance of changing one another's minds on such critical issues. After all, values
are a fundamental part of our identity. Probably the best choice
in confronting value conflicts is simply to agree to disagree about
these value issues. For example, abortion is a fairly fundamental
value conflict regarding freedom of choice and right to life. As
long as the dispute involves these deeply held values, the dispute
will rage on. Neither side has much chance of changing the other
side's mind. Each side uses a variety of techniques to impose its
perspective. But the real conflict remains as long as each side refuses to respect the other's position.

COMMUNICATION SKILLS

Certainly, the type of issue in dispute and its importance, combined with the importance of the relationship, weigh heavily on the decision to confront the conflict. Let's assume that you decide that both the issue and the relationship are important. You should probably ask yourself some additional questions. For example, do both parties have the necessary communication skills to work through the conflict? Some research dealing with aggressiveness (Infante, 1987) reveals that people with impaired communication skills resort first to aggressiveness and then to violence. People need communication skills to listen to others, develop proposals, and bargain about interests. Communication skill differences become a real problem when parties try to confront their conflicts constructively.

CONFLICT STYLE

Another important factor determining how parties might deal with conflict relates to their conflict style. Kilmann and Thomas (1975) identify five different styles people might use when approaching conflict based on concern for their own and the other's interests (Table 2.1). As this model indicates, showing low concern for one's own and the other's interests reflects an *avoiding* style of handling conflict. Under these conditions, individuals feel little motivation to proceed because confronting the conflict offers little hope of satisfying the parties' needs. However, if individuals remain unconcerned about their own needs but become very concerned about the other's, then they pursue an *accommodating* style. They give in most of the time, and sacrifice their own needs. Some individuals pursue just the opposite style involving a high concern for their own needs and low concern for the others'. This *competing* style becomes most prevalent when the issues begin to turn toward value and relational concerns in which protecting personal needs becomes a big priority.

Perhaps the style requiring the most communicative skill involves *collaborating* with the other party. This style demonstrates high concern for both parties: I want my needs satisfied, but I want the other to be satisfied as well. The reason this style requires the

Table 2.1 Kilmann and Thomas Conflict Styles

	High	Competition	Collaboration
Concern			
for		Compromise	
Self			
	Low	Avoidance	Accommodation
		Low	High
		Concern for Other	

most communication skill is that both parties must reveal their needs and then construct creative ways of satisfying those needs.

For example, consider a divorcing couple fighting over the custody of their children. If they both used a collaborative style in handling the conflict then each party would talk about several issues. Specifically, the couple would talk about why each person wanted custody and how each of these needs might be worked into some kind of agreement. This approach requires more information sharing than any other style and, as a result, requires more time and energy from the couple.

When people show some concern for their own needs and some concern for the other's needs, they engage in *compromising*. Usually, many people cite this style as the most desirable, but when you think about it, compromising involves both parties settling for just some of what they want. It is certainly easier to split the difference on a problem than to spend time inventing a collaborative solution benefiting both parties.

Some additional points about style bear discussion. First, people probably need all five styles at different points in a conflict. Sometimes competing works to motivate the other to get involved in the conflict. Or temporarily accommodating someone might give him or her time to calm down and think. Clearly, no one style is always best.

Second, you have probably noticed that the more you move toward collaboration, the more concern you show for the relationship. After all, when people show concern for one another's needs, they express a desire to improve their relationship as well. Perhaps you thought that accommodators showed the most concern for the relationship, because they were willing to do anything to try to please the other person. Actually, by denying your own needs, you make it difficult to achieve a satisfying relationship because both parties are not contributing fully to that relationship. Thus full-time accommodators should carefully evaluate their preference in terms of its long-term value.

Finally, culture enters the picture as an important factor in determining a person's desire to confront a conflict. For example, confrontation or any kind of conflict in many Asian cultures communicates lack of respect for that person. In many American cultures, people consider not confronting a conflict as a lack of interest or courage. Before expecting someone to confront a problem, always consider whether that person's culture encourages or discourages conflict confrontation.

TIME

Another factor to consider in your confrontation decision making is time. When people perceive time closing in on them, they are more likely to confront the conflict than avoid it. For example, I feel that telling a friend about a problem before he or she learns about it from others is generally the best policy. The possibility of my friend learning about the problem very soon imposes a time deadline on me to confront the problem with the friend right away. The key in dealing with time is to work toward expanding the amount of time available to deal with the problem. More time gives people a greater opportunity to calm down and to plan how they wish to work together. Imposing time demands on someone sends a highly competitive message to that other person. Hostage negotiators indicate that time is their best friend. When they lengthen the negotiation process, the other party calms down and becomes much more willing to bargain.

PERSONAL SAFETY

Finally, consider personal safety when making your confrontation decisions. If engaging in the conflict may cause you personal harm, then avoidance is mandatory. Many women are victims of spouse abuse because their husbands or male friends cannot handle conflicts with verbal communication, they only know violence. Under such circumstances, personal safety is a key decision, particularly when the conflict escalates to the fight/flight level.

A CLASSIC EXAMPLE

The list of factors that affect your decision to confront the conflict must appear fairly unreasonable or unrealistic to you (Table 2.2). In truth, how often do people take these factors into account? The answer is probably not that often. That is the reason most people are not very effective conflict managers. If they took the time to think about these factors, they might find themselves working through conflict more effectively.

Consider the following example of a student's account of a conflict she experienced recently with her boyfriend:

> My boyfriend is mad because he wants me to spend the night at his place more often, and I don't want to. He's mad that I haven't stayed there the past two nights and now he is "uninviting" me to stay tonight. He said that he's not just going to sit around and wait until it is convenient for me to stay there. He claims that it is not "convenient" for me to stay there tonight.

This is a classic example of a couple in the throes of relational growing pains. They are unsure about whether, or how, to escalate the relationship. They have initiated a very physically intimate relationship but now their emotions and their communications need to catch up somehow. It appears that neither is ready to confront the real issue about how they really feel about each other and what to do about the relationship.

❏ Decision 2: When Should I Confront the Conflict?

PLANNING

Many people might view this question with some skepticism. Perhaps few people ever think about when to confront a conflict

Table 2.2 Evaluating Your Confrontation Decisions

The purpose of this questionnaire is to help you decide if you should confront a conflict. Think about a major problem you have with another person right now. Should you confront the conflict or let it alone? To find out, check your answers to the following questions.

	A	B
1. Is your relationship with this other person important to you?	No_____	Yes_____
2. Is the issue in dispute important to you?	No_____	Yes_____
3. Do you become verbally aggressive during conflict?	Yes_____	No_____
4. Do you look for ways to use a collaborative conflict style in resolving your disputes?	No_____	Yes_____
5. Is the amount of time available to deal with the problem limited?	Yes_____	No_____
6. Do you fear for your personal safety if you confront the problem?	Yes_____	No_____

To find your score, count your check marks in column B. If you had four or more, then you should, and can, confront the problem. Who knows, perhaps you will learn something important about yourself if you take the risk and confront the problem.

other than saying to themselves, "I'll wait till he's in a good mood, then I'll tell him about it." As it turns out, timing and planning are important parts of productive conflict management. Certainly, you can rush into the dispute and say anything that comes to mind. But when people are not ready to talk, communication can make the problem worse. The girlfriend and boyfriend problem about staying overnight begs for exposure. They now must decide when to confront it.

The key to timing is planning.

The key to timing is planning. Planning is difficult when another person confronts you with a conflict. Most of us deal with it at that moment instead of postponing the problem until a better time. However, when you decide to confront someone else about a problem, planning becomes a more realistic option. Then we take time to consider the best approach in dealing with the other person.

Does taking the time to plan how confrontation occurs make any difference in how well the conflict turns out? Some research in the international arena (Herek, Janis, & Huth, 1989) indicates that effective planning is much more likely to determine outcome than the severity of the problem. When parties gather information systematically and consider and reconsider their options, they are much more likely to be effective. Research in negotiation confirms this finding. Roloff and Jordan (1991) discovered that planning before a negotiation greatly increases the bargainer's ability to achieve his or her high profit goals.

These studies support the need for planning. Even easy problems can be messed up quickly if people fail to use the proper approach to deal with the problem. The proper planning approach involves gathering information about your options, considering and reconsidering options, and learning as much about the other as possible. You probably noticed that the decisions about whether or not to confront a conflict are quite detailed and fairly extensive. The point is that wading through those issues gives you a much better chance to make the right decision about confronting the problem. Making quick decisions on limited information quickly gets you into problems.

THE IMPORTANT TIMING CONSIDERATIONS

Emotions

What are the important considerations in deciding when to confront a conflict? First, consider emotions, yours and the other person's. When either you or the other person becomes really angry, hurt, or intensely emotional in other ways, is confrontation useful at that point? Can either of you really listen to the other's position?

To answer this question, consider this conflict. Just before last Christmas, a group of public school fifth graders wanted to participate in a school play about the birth of Jesus. The play did not specifically include the Christmas characters, but the story mirrored it in a more contemporary setting. Several non-Christian parents objected to the play in a public school even though none of the characters portrayed Christians. Christian parents became quite angry with the objecting parents and the issue became quite emotional. Each side started yelling at the other during a school meeting.

Unfortunately, the school failed to develop a policy about presenting these kinds of plays. Should the principal have tried to develop such a policy during the Christmas season when emotions were peaked? Wisely, the principal decided to cancel the play for that year and try to develop a policy for such plays after the Christmas season ended. Clearly, the community needed time to consider the issue in detail. Delaying the discussion until emotions cooled proved wise, because the community took its time and developed an intelligent policy for dealing with plays that had religious overtones.

Confronting problems when individuals express intense emotions is generally counterproductive. People are too defensive when trying to protect their personal needs to concentrate on the substantive issues. The parents' emotions stemmed from threats aimed at their religious freedom of expression. They needed to get past their defensive orientations before being able to focus on substantive issues. However, as we will learn in the next chapter, sometimes parties need to stimulate emotions to make them sufficiently motivated to focus on the real issues. When emotions render people out of control, generally time is needed to calm the parties down before addressing their concerns (Table 2.3).

Time Pressures

What if postponing the conflict until a later time is not possible? For example, someone might confront you with a problem and want to talk about it immediately. When the other person is ready to discuss a problem but you are too emotional or unprepared to consider the problem, you must weigh the decision carefully. If the confronter might not bring up the conflict again if you

Table 2.3 Assessing Your Emotions in a Conflict Situation

The purpose of this questionnaire is to help you assess your emotions in a conflict. Respond to each statement by indicating the degree to which the statement is true for you.

   If you "Never" act in the described manner, answer 1;

   if you "Almost Never" act in the described manner, answer 2;

   if you "Sometimes" act in the described manner, answer 3;

   if you "Almost Always" act in the described manner, answer 4;

   if you "Always" act in the described manner, answer 5.

When I must confront a conflict, I

_____ feel uncomfortable.

_____ become angry.

_____ feel stress.

_____ become sad.

_____ feel scared.

To find your score, add the numbers you wrote next to each item. Scores will range from 5 to 25. The higher your score, the more emotionally unprepared you are to confront conflict.

refuse to talk about it, then confronting it immediately might be the best choice. Often it takes a great deal of courage for others to discuss a sensitive topic. If you put them off, they may not bring it up again, and an opportunity to clear the air might be lost.

The following conflict account written by a female student illustrates a typical timing problem:

> I fought with my boyfriend when he was drunk (I was not). He misunderstood why I was talking to a girlfriend about her prob-lems. I ended up walking off with my friend and we didn't see my boyfriend or her boyfriend again that night. The conflict continued into the next day and he ended up punching through the glass in the front door because I wouldn't let him in.

The student decided not to fight with her boyfriend while he was drunk. It is generally not a good idea to argue with someone with impaired thinking abilities. However, the boyfriend took the confrontation fairly far the next day and became quite violent. Should the student have confronted the boyfriend while he was violent? Again, he experienced impaired thinking, so perhaps she made the right decision. Could they ever develop an ability to sit down and confront their concerns constructively?

❑ Decision 3: How Should I Confront the Conflict?

After deciding to confront the conflict and when to make your move, the next step involves deciding how to manage the conflict when it begins. What strategies work best? In general, the kinds of strategies you need depend on the kind of conflict that results from the confrontation. The reactions of the parties you decide to confront might involve a willingness to explore the problem. This reaction places the conflict in the problems-to-solve category, discussed in Chapter 1. In this type of conflict, people avoid violating one another's personal needs while focusing on the issues. When the confrontation produces this kind of productive reaction, you enter the negotiation phase of the dispute; Chapter 6 discusses negotiation in detail.

However, what if your confrontation escalates the conflict to a much more difficult level? For example, let's assume it places you in the fight/flight level of conflict. How can you transform this situation into a more productive discussion? To make this transformation, it is necessary to *manage the crisis first*. How can you respond to people who are out of control and exhibit signs of being in a crisis? Recall the student with the drunken, violent boyfriend? She faced the problem of figuring out how to respond to this person who wanted to fight violently. Then, once the crisis is managed, how do you create a structure that keeps the conflict from escalating once again? Let's try to answer these important questions.

CRISIS DEFINED

During fight/flight conflict, resistance becomes intense and the underlying assumption of the conflict moves away from

cooperation, toward competition. The other party has no intention of wanting to get along. He or she has become stupid, has lost
control, and simply wants to fight. Recall that these conflicts generally threaten individuals' personal needs. So the person in crisis
will do anything necessary, often at any cost, to protect those needs.

When the confrontation places people in this kind of conflict,
they find themselves in crisis. Three criteria distinguish a crisis from
other kinds of events.

1. Individuals challenge one another's personal needs.
2. The situation generally catches these individuals by surprise in the
   sense that they could not see the event coming.
3. Because parties threaten personal needs, and the event limits time
   to plan or think, normal problem-solving practices break down or
   remain unavailable to the parties in conflict. (It is important to
   restrict the focus to crises that involve individuals in conflict with
   others as opposed to individuals in conflict with themselves.)

For example, in hostage negotiations, parties are in crisis because each party challenges the other's high-priority personal
needs. Furthermore, the situation catches at least one party by
surprise, and the hostage takers obviously believe that normal
problem- solving activities cannot satisfy their personal needs. In
one hostage incident a man hijacked a plane to show his girlfriend that he was "a man." She had just broken up with him, and
he wanted to demonstrate his courage. The police finally persuaded
him to release the passengers after the girlfriend acknowledged
the hostage taker's bravado in hijacking the airplane. His main
goal was confirmation of a deep personal need to be seen as a
powerful person.

ELEMENTS OF CRISIS COMMUNICATION

How do you know when someone is in crisis? You might look
for several elements.

1. Are parties trying to threaten or coerce one another to get their way?
2. Are emotions coming quickly to the surface of the discussion? In
   crisis people openly express fear, hostility, resentment and other
   emotions indicating a violation of personal needs.

3. Are the parties using strategies intended to protect their self-esteem? Defensive reactions such as excuses and justifications qualify as attempts to save face.

4. Is there a sense of urgency in the discussion? People struggle vigorously to resolve crises very quickly because they want the problem to go away immediately. As a result, they fail to evaluate options carefully. Instead, they try to impose their most preferred option on others at the first opportunity. As suggested in Chapter 1, crises gain a life of their own. Like a runaway freight train, the rush of events remains marginally subject to control.

If you find the conflict displaying these features, then you might face a very difficult crisis. If so, you do not want to make the crisis worse by further antagonizing the individuals. For example, the most common mistake people make when confronting a crisis situation is to move too quickly to impose a solution on what appears to be the problem. When in crisis, people are not generally ready for problem solving. They need to have their emotions calmed first to prepare them for this *thinking* and not *feeling* transition.

To illustrate this idea, consider a man who expressed his frustration at not being able to communicate with his daughter when she was in crisis. He desperately wanted to help, but she continuously rejected his offers. When asked to describe how he advises her, he recalled his professional expertise.

When I get to work I have 20 phone calls from 20 people with 20 crises and I have only 20 minutes to solve all these crises. So I get on the phone and tell people what they need to do to solve their problem. Since I have only 1 minute, I don't have time to hold their hand.

When asked why he thought this process did not work for his daughter, he had no idea. After all, he gave her great suggestions about how to solve her problems. He is the pro at problem solving, and all he needs is 1 minute! I indicated that when people are in crisis, their first need is for someone to *listen* to their problems. By talking out the problems, people make sense out of them and feel like the listener really cares about them. The father failed to allow his daughter to vent her frustrations so she believed he didn't care about, and thus did not respect, her problems. In other words, she perceived that he violated her personal needs, which actually intensified the crisis for her.

Unfortunately, this problem of not listening to concerns and then trying to impose solutions is quite common, particularly for men talking to women. Men typically show little interest in listening to women's concerns. They often try to end the discussion by imposing solutions even when the woman is not interested in actually solving the problem but instead wants to talk about it. When she fails to act on his solutions, the man becomes more angry and frustrated and seeks to escape from the situation. This scenario represents a common way in which conflicts escalate into crises for couples.

COMMUNICATION STRATEGIES FOR
MOVING OUT OF CRISIS

Your basic communication goal in a crisis involves controlling aggressive, needs-centered interaction patterns. It means moving away from a focus on satisfying overwhelming personal needs for safety or respect toward a focus on personal interests. This objective recalls the definition of conflict from Chapter 1: *A situation in which interdependent people express differences in satisfying their individual needs and interests, and they experience interference from each other in accomplishing these goals.* Fighting over individual needs quickly escalates into crisis, because these needs are not negotiable for most people. However, interests are negotiable. As a result, moving away from needs and toward interests represents the key communication challenge in which people can then discuss the issues disturbing them.

Several communication strategies work well in focusing the discussion on substantive issues. First, people in crisis need emotional reflection. This involves labeling the emotion for the person and recognizing that you understand that the person is emotional. Labeling both shows support for the person's right to have feelings about the situation and helps the person better understand his or her feelings. Remember, feelings are difficult to understand and people need guidance in this effort. Denying the other's emotion (like the father did by moving too quickly to solutions) demonstrates resistance and only places the other further into crisis.

This reflection process is really the first form of empathy. Empathy involves perspective taking, or showing understanding for the other's experience. Some people call this *putting yourself in the other person's shoes*. There are two principal kinds of empathic behavior. At the most basic level, the person simply listens or provides some positive response to the other person. Reflecting is a good example of this kind of empathy. Other active listening techniques such as repeating the other's comments and/or asking them to go on are good examples of basic empathy. At a more complex level, empathy involves giving messages of support to the other person. These messages might involve sharing your own experiences on similar problems or elaborating on the other's feelings. Any explicit form of acceptance shows empathy for the other's concerns.

The *Four R Method* is a useful guide for escaping crises:

1. *Receive* the other's comments without interruption and don't get defensive. Receiving shows caring and is the first phase of empathic listening.
2. *Repeat* the person's comments as objectively as possible. Repeating can encourage the person to open up about the problem and can include reflecting and discussing the other person's emotions.
3. *Request* the other's proposed ways of dealing with the problem. Requesting is third because people in crisis are not capable of beginning with solutions. They need to begin with emotional release and a discussion of their problem.
4. *Review* the options and decide on the best approach.

This basic four-step approach helps the other move away from emotional concerns because you avoid challenging the person along the way. Remember, people in crisis cannot think. They get stupid. By moving slowly toward requesting information, you allow people time to calm down and start thinking about their problem.

Focusing on interests *after* emotions constitutes another good way for defusing a crisis. The first two R's, receiving and repeating, aim to satisfy personal needs and help you show interest and commitment without encouraging defensiveness or resistance. The next two R's, requesting and reviewing, try to move the inter-action toward interests. Asking questions about the problem and then reviewing options constitute the essence of problem solving. If you can move to that point, you have succeeded in moving away from a crisis and to-ward a problem-solving situation in which only interests divide parties. At that point, parties have only one prob-lem to deal with—interests—and not two problems—emotions and interests.

Deal first with emotion and second with substance.

What happens when people are not in crisis? What about just the run-of-the-mill conflicts that you might see every day? Han-dling people in crisis is certainly the most difficult conflict-han-dling skill, so that skill needs special attention. But when people have fewer severe reactions to confrontation, these same rules apply. *Deal first with emotion and second with substance.* Take your time. It is possible to use the Four R Method in most any kind of conflict situation.

STRUCTURAL MEANS FOR MOVING OUT OF CRISES

Chapter 7 discusses options for help when one-on-one negoti-ation fails. Calling in mediators, arbitrators, or some other kinds of counselors generally yields impressive results. One big reason they work is structure. Recall that in crisis, normal structures for problem solving have broken down. The individual feels that only aggression, and not cooperation, can solve the problem. When in-dividuals lose a structure for solving their problems, they need to rely on others to supply that structure. For example, the court sys-tem is the best-known structure for handling disputes. In fact, it is the final structure. When people's informal means of working through their problems fail, the courts must deal with the problems.

The point is that we need rules for problem solving. Rules give people guidance so they refrain from doing something that is not constructive. That is, rules prevent people from getting stupid. Of course, too many rules constrain individuality and creativity;

too few rules can lead to anarchy. Do you have rules for your conflicts? A friend described a rule her parents used when fighting: "Never go to bed angry." Sometimes they stayed up late, but they always went to bed with their conflicts resolved.

Do you think the couple that was involved in the dispute that resulted in a punched-out door enjoyed a good set of rules for fighting? In all likelihood, they had few, if any, established rules for fighting. Uncontrolled escalation seemed the preferred choice.

A good point to remember is that even if you do not think you use any rules when fighting, you do. Think about the patterns of communication you use when fighting with a friend or parent. Do they reflect some rules that you can identify? The final section of this chapter talks about some conflict patterns that reflect rules for fighting. See if you find any that are familiar.

❑ Types of Conflict Cycles

When people choose to confront a conflict, what are some typical patterns of escalation and deescalation? How might using the Four R Method help manage these situations? Let's review these patterns to learn how conflict evolves.

SKIRTING

A popular conflict cycle aims at trying to skirt or dodge the important issues by focusing only on the less-controversial problems. This cycle begins with a confrontation and ends with the other person changing the topic, making a joke about the situation, or even leaving. Skirting is a form of avoidance. You have probably witnessed families quite skilled at skirting important issues. When an important issue arises, they choose not to acknowledge it or wait for a more opportune time to deal with the conflict. They seek only to avoid difficulty.

PERSONALIZING

Relationships can become strained when confrontation begins. Often this strain results in a personalizing cycle that begins with a confrontation that focuses on some personal quality of the other person. For example, the individual might begin the confrontation with the comment, "Why are you always so aggressive?" Negatively labeling someone's personality certainly forces them into a defensive position, because the negative label attacks the other's personal need for a positive self-image. In fact, few people like to have others evaluate their personality because such evaluations are like saying, "You are bad, and you can't do anything about it." This forces the other person into a corner and nearly guarantees the defensive reaction. We will learn in Chapter 3 that personalizing a conflict in this manner is one of the most common and unconstructive cycles identified in the literature.

Along with making personality evaluations, a personalizing cycle can begin with a mind-reading statement. The person might say, "I know you hate me." How do you respond when people tell you how you think? Most people take offense at mind-reading comments because they impose thoughts on us we might not be thinking. Again, mind reading is another form of backing someone into a corner. Personalizing a conflict leads to a defensive cycle that can end up focusing only on relational issues.

COMPLAINING

Complaining loops begin when someone confronts another person with some kind of accusation. Research on complaining comes largely from the marital communication literature (Fitzpatrick, 1989). Although it pertains mostly to married couples, the loop still appears in other kinds of conflicts. The loop goes something like this:

1. One party confronts the other and shows anger or sends some other kind of negative feeling message. Usually, in a marriage, the wife initiates the confrontation with a comment that clearly shows her emotions.
2. The other party, generally the husband, avoids the conflict with statements of denial or topic avoidance or shifting levels of abstraction. Husbands, particularly in unhappy marriages, become quite practiced at avoiding conflicts.
3. The first party escalates with more accusations.

4. The second party continues to avoid.
5. This response sends the first party out of control. They get stupid. They become very upset at this point, because of the avoidance.
6. This outburst generally results in the second party leaving the scene in a flight response.

Recent research in marital communication indicates that this kind of sequence needs to be interrupted as soon as possible (Donohue, 1991). When others (generally conflict professionals) sense that parties are not sensitive to one another's emotions, they strive to label these emotions and block paths of denial and avoidance. Be careful of this cycle, because it is quite common and becomes an easy trap for intimate couples to fall into.

SNIPING

Have you ever witnessed someone taking a cheap shot at another person and then running away? This is called sniping. That is, individuals make a negative comment through an indirect question or hostile joking, and then exit the scene. The other has no chance to respond or to expose the important issues in dispute. This sniping/exit cycle is again common in intimate situations, because couples demonstrate an inability to get past their relational problems and focus instead on their real concerns.

AGGRESSING

Aggressing appears repeatedly in this book because understanding all the ways aggression can enter our lives is important. In the classic cycle, individuals use verbal aggression to protect their identities and their personal need to be viewed in a positive way. This verbal aggression sequence evolves like this:

1. A norm violation occurs. Someone calls another person a bad name or makes an offensive remark.
2. The attacked person immediately examines the situational factors such as who else is present and their sex and role. Research dealing with spouse abuse (Felson, 1984) tells us that escalation intensifies in response to attacks in front of people of the same sex and of higher status than the person under attack.

3. The attacked person asks the other to explain the violation to determine the other's intention. Why did the person do this? Was it a mistake, or was it intentional?

4. If the person determines that the other really meant what he or she said and the audience is passive, the person will try some kind of verbal or physical aggression to repair the loss of face. Again, the violation of personal needs brings very swift and decisive reactions.

VALIDATING

The final cycle has more to do with couples succeeding in dealing with their problems. Gottman (1979) finds that happily married couples experience what he calls a validation sequence. Validation involves confirming or supporting the other's self-worth or identity. This cycle begins the same way as the complaining loop, except that the second party uses the Four R Method. They first *receive* the other's comments and listen for emotion. Having spotted emotion, they *repeat* the comments to reflect the emotion and, in the process, validate the person's right to have an emotional experience. They then *request* more information about the problem and *review* options to generate satisfactory options. The cycle turns away from a complaining loop quickly. The second person does not ignore or avoid the upset person but, instead, tries to work with the concern and profit from the experience.

❑ Conclusions

Detecting patterns of communication is a difficult process. You can see unusual patterns all the time if you look for them. You can also train your eyes and ears to detect patterns that either help or hinder relational growth. For example, a friend recently commented on an interesting communication pattern in her home. She remarked that her family constantly interrupts one another. They have trouble completing their thoughts. However, on closer inspection, it was clear that the pattern was more elaborate than simple interruption. Apparently, each person receives a talking turn, but the person gets only about seven words to say whatever he or she desires. At the end of the seven words, the listeners interrupt the speaker and completely change the topic. This "seven-word rule" troubled the student; yet the student failed to notice the rule. But what really troubled her most was her inability to solve conflicts or disclose intimate information with her family. After all, how can you solve problems or express concerns with only seven words?

Consider these final thoughts about the ideas in this chapter. First, it should be obvious that confronting is very difficult. It takes lots of courage even to make the decision in most cases. Making the decision to confront generally proves productive and worth the effort. You probably won't believe that until you read the rest of the book, but current evidence suggests that confronting, as a rule, works better than avoiding. Again, there are some notable exceptions, particularly with respect to timing or the threat of personal safety. But in the most common conflict situation, confrontation works.

Second, planning smooths the process considerably. Well-planned confrontations work out much better than unplanned ones. How much time should you spend planning? Consider the slogan, "There never seems to be enough time to do the job right, but always time to do it over." Planning asks you to invest your time on the front end of the problem as opposed to the back end. Waiting until the problem grows large requires significantly more repair work than a little routine maintenance up front.

Third, remain sensitive to conflict cycles that can arise when confronting. Learn to avoid patterns that can lead to crises. If the other person seems to be in crisis, take your time and try not to make the situation worse. Be vigilant in looking for patterns that might help or hinder the conflict management process.

3

Face Saving

The last chapter stressed the need to confront conflict and to prepare for the emotional disruption that often follows confrontation. In fact, most of us fear conflict because of the possibility of this kind of emotional outburst. The general goal laid out in the last chapter focuses on understanding some key elements that can fan the flames of crisis if left unattended.

The goal of this chapter is to elaborate on two remaining elements that, if handled improperly, can further toss people into crisis. Those issues are *attribution* and *face*. Attribution explores how people perceive the causes of conflict; face examines how people's identities, or self-images affect their ability to work through a crisis. This chapter begins with the attribution issue, moves to a discussion of face, and concludes with some strategies for managing the attribution/face problem.

❏ The Attribution of Cause Question

When we first plunge into conflict, do we typically focus on ideas we share in common or on ideas that divide us? Certainly, most conflicts begin with a focus on differences. Folger and Poole (1984) call this initial period of conflict the *differentiation* phase in which parties concentrate on problems or issues that make them different. Think of your last conflict. You probably began by pointing out how the other party was doing something that you did not like. The focus was on differences. You certainly could have started talking about those things that you have in common: your shared values about the relationship and spending time together. But most people begin conflicts by using differentiation strategies.

To illustrate this point, let's return to the student's problem about her boyfriend punching out the front door. As they yelled at each other through the door, she noted that the following issues arose:

1. "He thought I was sleeping with another guy the night before."
2. "He called me names and belittled me."
3. "He didn't trust me."
4. "He is very immature."

Here we see evidence of classic differentiation. The parties focus on differences in the course of fighting about their concerns. This conflict may not have enjoyed any movement toward integrating positions and focusing on joint gains.

Folger and Poole (1984) point out that if parties successfully work through their differences, they reach an *integration* phase. During this phase, parties merge positions in an attempt to emphasize joint gains. The goal is for both parties to build a cooperative process that allows them to find a common ground, so ideally both sides can accomplish their goals. Pruitt (1981) lists several integrative strategies that individuals can use to help each other accomplish their goals. One very useful strategy he calls *cost-cutting*. Parties help one another overcome any problems that might arise as a result of the negotiation. A second strategy, *bridging*, involves designing some third creative alternative that bridges the parties' individual goals. Whatever type of integrative method people use, they show a commitment to move beyond differences and focus on solving their problem.

So, for most conflicts, reaching the point of integration requires getting through the differentiation phase. Unfortunately, during this phase, people typically use what might be called *finger-pointing* tactics. That is, each party points its finger at the other and says, "You did this and you did that *because* you are . . ." Then he or she brings up some kind of problem the other person has. Does this sound familiar? If you described your last conflict, you would probably try to lay all the blame on the other person: He or she *caused* the problem.

Take comfort in the knowledge that this reaction typifies the way most people deal with conflict. In fact, when we begin discussions of differences, we constantly search for reasons to explain why the conflict arose in the first place. Perhaps attribution theory can provide us with some insights about how this thought process works. We certainly need to know more about the factors that help us to—and prevent us from—moving toward integration.

BASIC PRINCIPLES OF ATTRIBUTION THEORY

Attribution theory focuses on two main issues associated with how people view change (see Fiske & Taylor, 1984, for a description). First, consider the issue of responsibility. Who or what is ultimately responsible for changes in the world? Do I cause things to change or are others responsible for change? Second is the issue of anticipated reactions. Is the other person likely to respond cooperatively or competitively when confronted with conflict? The best approach is to look at these issues separately to understand their impact in moving from a differentiation to an integration phase in conflict.

The Responsibility Issue

Recall from the last two chapters that external threats to our personal needs stimulate a need for protection. We want to protect our values, freedoms, and power positions from disruption. We also want to keep our face, or self-image, intact. In fact, protecting against face threats is a high priority.

Attribution theory says that one of the primary ways we protect ourselves is to bias our perceptions of the causes of conflict.

Our natural tendency is to think that the other person is the cause of the conflict. How many times have you seen yourself as simply an innocent bystander minding your own business until that other person came along and created all the problems? You can see how this biasing serves as a self-protector. We certainly try to avoid thinking we are the problem. That admission requires changing important personal needs.

When we attribute the cause of conflict to the other person, we go one step further. We work to figure out why the other person is causing all these problems. In general, we select from two possible causes. First, something about the *situation, or something external to the individual,* could have caused him or her to act in a particular way. Perhaps the person came from a strange family. Or someone may have forced or tricked the person into causing the problem. These factors are beyond the individual's personal control. Second, we can point to some kind of *disposition, or personal quality,* that could have determined the individual's behavior. The person caused the problems because he or she is insecure, stupid, lazy, or insensitive, for example. These factors are under the individual's personal control.

Fundamental Attribution Error: We focus on the personal traits and not the situational traits.

When we pick between the two to identify the cause of the conflict, which do you think we tend to select? Research reveals that people tend to pick personal dispositional qualities and ignore the situational influences. How often have you said, "So and so did this or that to me because she's just too insecure to deal with me," or "He's just too aggressive to get along with people." Researchers term this bias the *fundamental attribution error.* We focus on the personal traits and not the situational traits. For example, a student provided this list of causes to describe a conflict with her stepfather about an impending divorce from her mother:

1. "He treats my mom badly."
2. "He lies to me."
3. "He tries to control me."

4. "He tries to lecture me too much."
5. "He has no respect for anyone but himself."

Do you see all the dispositional attributions? The stepdad is controlling, self-centered, and disrespectful. Do you also focus on the other's dispositional qualities when trying to understand your conflicts? Most people commit this fundamental attribution error when trying to decide how to manage a conflict.

But why do you focus on personalities and not situational features? What motivates this bias in the way you perceive conflict? This bias satisfies your need for self-protection. Focusing on the other person's personal qualities eliminates your responsibility in contributing to the conflict. You heap the blame squarely on the other's shoulders to preserve your self-image as a good, honest individual. Focusing on situational causes does not accomplish this self-preservation goal as well, because the personal qualities are under the individual's control. However, the individual does not control the various situational factors that can cause conflict. As a result, the situational factors are not as effective in heaping the blame on the other person. Making the other person fully responsible for the conflict keeps your self-image intact.

How do you respond when people lay all the blame on your personal attributes? Most people get angry because nobody likes to hear that he or she is personally deficient. Again, this violates a personal need and thus stimulates unproductive conflicts. We know from marital communication literature that when people focus on personality conflicts, couples see their problems as fundamentally irreconcilable. Personality factors are not negotiable.

Interestingly, conflicts can start more productively if people focus not on personalities but on factors that do not threaten individual needs. For example, individuals' goals and perceptions or uncontrollable situational factors could have contributed to the problem. Simple misunderstandings, resulting from faulty interaction patterns, can also cause destructive conflicts. If people identify such causes at the beginning of conflicts, they can do something about them. These factors are changeable. Personality traits are not changeable. So focusing on other causes is the beginning of more productive conflict management.

Several recent studies confirm difficulties caused by committing the fundamental attribution error. For example, people that attribute the conflict's cause to the other person tend to use more avoidance and competitive interaction strategies. They use avoidance tactics because the person can't change anyway, so why try to do something about the conflict? They use competitive tactics because they are trying to change things that are not changeable. People take offense at challenges to our personal attributes. Again, like the student experiencing her parent's divorce, we need to protect ourselves. So we either avoid the conflict or we get involved and try to force the others to change their personalities.

However, when people attribute the cause, or at least some of the cause of the conflict, to themselves, they use more integrative strategies. Think about it. If you feel you contributed to the problem, you are more willing to listen to the other side and consider his or her point of view. Remember your last conflict in which you took some of the blame for the problem? You were probably more willing to listen and to solve the problem. For example, in alcoholic treatment programs, one of the first goals for family members of alcoholic parties is to recognize their role in supporting the alcoholic's problem. They must see their own contributions to the problem before they are able to help.

Anticipated Reactions

In addition to thinking about who caused the conflict, attribution theory also says that we create expectations about future events. For example, we wonder how the other person will react to our confrontation or to our particular strategies. A friend was talking recently about getting a divorce. She kept wondering what her husband was going to do when she told him she wanted a divorce. "What will he do when I say I want out?" Research reveals that we generally see others as more competitive that ourselves. We believe they will overreact but that we see the situation in a much more cooperative way. Have you ever thought, "Gee, I just know they are going to hit the ceiling when I tell them that"?

Why do we form such expectations about others? Quite simply, we search for likely reactions as a means of predicting how effective our own conflict management strategies might be. Will our strategies yield effective or ineffective results? When we believe we can be very successful, then we are more likely to try some kind of conflict resolution attempt. Perhaps we might use a competitive, collaborative, or even a compromise strategy. But we must believe that we can do something about the conflict.

So when our expectations for success are high, we are more likely to persist in attempts to resolve conflicts. Conversely, when we hold low expectations of success, we tend to avoid conflicts. Analyze your last conflict avoidance incident. Did you believe that it simply was not worth the trouble because the other person was not likely to change anyway?

Several factors appear to affect our expectations of success in conflict. First, when we attribute the source of the problem to the other's personality, then our expectations of success tend to drop. We see that the other person's personality is a stable problem and one that is unlikely to change. So why bother trying to do anything about the conflict?

Second, when people feel committed to the relationship, they are more likely to hold high expectations of success. The primary reason is that relationships can be changed or influenced in some way. We choose not to view them as unchangeable, like someone's personality. So if parties want to hold on, and they believe that relationships can be improved, then they believe that their strategies will work.

COMMUNICATION AND ATTRIBUTION

How does communication affect the kinds of attributions individuals form? This question is certainly important for conflict managers. Communication is the medium we use to manage conflict in most instances. One important issue relates to information exchange. Research indicates that exchanging information reduces the potential for false attributions, because the information serves to reduce ambiguity in the situation.

For example, suppose you get angry with a colleague because he failed to meet you for an appointment, and you never talked to him about his tardiness. Your first tendency is to blame his personal trait of tardiness. "Oh, he's just lazy and probably forgot to write down the appointment." If you don't talk to him about the problem and you just assume it's because of his personality, you probably will continue to avoid the problem. You conclude that you can't change him anyway. However, if you asked him about the problem and he revealed that he had an emergency and could not possibly contact you, then you could correct your false attribution about the person.

The lesson is clear. Exchanging information really helps constructive problem solving. Unfortunately, when people get mad at others, their first tendency is to close down communication, which only adds to the problem in most cases.

Self-disclosure also increases integrative problem solving because it provides better information about the causes of conflict. When you learn personal information about someone, you are more likely to give that person a break than to assume automatically that they want to act competitively toward you. I certainly respond better to people when they are willing to tell me something about themselves. In fact, when I learn that others are human, I start to think about my responsibility in the conflict. After all, every conflict has two sides. What is my responsibility in this dispute? How much do I have to change to make this relationship work?

Structuring the conflict also increases integrativeness. When people add structure to the conflict through rules or by asking a mediator to help, they can exchange information in a less-threatening context. This exchange promotes more accurate attributions and thus increases an individual's estimates of success in dealing with the dispute.

CONCLUSIONS

Two points about attribution are most important. First, remember that personality attributions cause problems. The more you can resist forming these attributions, the more you will select integrative solutions and believe they will be successful. If you insist on focusing on personalities, you invite the other to use threats, attacks, and other pressures to get his or her way.

Second, internal attributions that assume some responsibility for the conflict typically lead to productive problem solving. When people take some responsibility for the difficulties, they are more likely to learn something from the conflict. Their strategies tend to emphasize more information sharing and presentation of options. Only when an individual's self-concept is secure can the individual use internal attributions to resolve conflict (Table 3.1).

Remember, internal-external attribution influences your perceptions of success in handling conflict. By making the personality attribution, you send the message that you believe that the other person cannot change. At this point, helplessness sets in. You avoid the conflict, if possible. On the other hand, by taking some responsibility for the dispute, you see the problem as temporary and more capable of successful resolution. Something can be done about these problems.

❑ **Face Needs in Conflict**

When people believe that the other's personality caused the conflicts, they tend to create competitive conflicts. These attributions threaten personal needs and encourage people to use face-defending tactics. "Get in my face, and I'll get in yours," you might hear someone blurt this out when challenged on some personal need. *Face* is defined as the person's desire for a positive identity. People want to look good and want others to see them in a generally positive light. Some people might wrap up their identity in being "cool" or "macho" or "crass." Everyone's face needs are a little different. But the basic objective is to maintain some kind of identity that we can call face.

Face also includes improving or strengthening this identity. We often wish to make our face better looking in a sense. For example, professors maintain such face needs as appearing smart, competent, and perhaps interesting. They want to write more books and conduct more research to enhance their reputation, which, in turn, improves their face. Of course, if someone claims a professor is stupid, then the professor must defend his or her face.

Table 3.1 Assessing Your Understanding of Attribution Theory

The purpose of this questionnaire is to see how well you understand attribution theory and its impact on conflict. Read these comments from people, describing the causes of their conflicts. Check the statements that contain attributions that are most likely to lead toward *successful* conflict resolution:

1._____ "Maybe our relationship can't handle this pressure."
2._____ "Why doesn't he stop being so stubborn about this problem?"
3._____ "Why didn't I tell her how I felt about her problem?"
4._____ "He just doesn't understand me."
5._____ "I guess his parents made him avoid conflict too much."
6._____ "My reaction was probably uncalled for."
7._____ "I guess he just doesn't care about me."
8._____ "I forced the confrontation, but he overreacted."
9._____ "Was my timing bad in confronting this problem?"
10._____ "I can get pretty angry at times."

If you said that statements 1, 3, 6, 9, and 10 were productive, you were right. All the others contain personality attributions that paint the wrong face on the conflict. The productive statements open opportunities for change and show flexibility in creating solutions.

After all, the professor has spent many years trying to establish a reputation, or identity.

Scholars studying face also reference the role of "significant others" in face work. A significant other is someone whose opinion carries extra weight. Traditionally, parents, siblings, or other respected individuals serve as significant others to most of us. This role is important because our face needs grow in front of significant others. Keep this concept in mind as we discuss the role of face in conflict.

WHY IS FACE IMPORTANT?

Many conflict scholars indicate that maintaining face serves as an important resource for supporting one's position in the dispute.

For example, in the bargaining context, Walton and McKersie (1965) indicate that maintaining face helps preserve trustworthiness. So if another negotiator successfully challenges my identity, then others might question my trustworthiness. After all, if I am not who I pretend to be, then my credibility is suspect.

Losing face can result in dire consequences for negotiators.

Losing face can also result in other dire consequences for negotiators. Pruitt (1971) indicates that loss of face communicates increased weakness. If constituents or opponents no longer view the negotiator as a credible person, then they will not take the negotiator's offers and proposals seriously. As a result, opponents expect more concessions from a negotiator with a weakened face. Also, opponents indicate a greater willingness to retaliate against a negotiator with a weakened face, simply because that person becomes more vulnerable.

Research in violence and aggression referred to in Chapter 2 indicates that verbal aggression stems from face-protection motivations. When a person receives an insult in front of a significant other, or someone of the same sex, the person usually becomes defensive and verbally aggressive. People need to save face when others challenge that face, particularly in front of people that might cause some embarrassment.

TYPES OF FACE NEEDS

We can conclude from these studies that, indeed, face makes a difference. Controlling face seems tied into controlling outcome. Most people realize this relationship because most cultures give their members a fairly strong emphasis on face. Perhaps the best way to understand the different aspects of face is to ask what different types of face needs people pursue to accomplish their goals. For example, when you are trying to buy a new car, what kind of face needs might you have to get the best deal?

Wilson and Putnam (1990) identify four different face needs.

(1) Face Maintenance. Maintaining face involves preserving one's image as a competent, trustworthy person. The goal is to bolster

our face to make it less vulnerable to attack. These bolstering strategies can be viewed as building up "face currency" toward a particular issue to make us less vulnerable. Such face needs are particularly critical when we are in a situation that might threaten
our face. Good examples of situations for which building face
currency would be useful are when we are in conflict or when we
need to persuade people.

(2) Face Saving. Saving face involves repairing a damaged image
in response to real or imagined threats. Most face-saving efforts
come in response to attacks or some other kind of violation. Acts
of aggression often stem from the need to look tough after someone else made you look weak.

You might think of face saving as a defensive move, which can
typically take one of three forms. The individual might shift attention away from another person's actions that could possibly
threaten face. Perhaps the best example of this strategy is changing the topic. People often change topics to avoid subjects that
may cause them to lose face. Second, the attacked person might
simply deny or reject the other's attack. Many politicians use this
strategy and often couple it with another attack to move from the
offensive to the defensive. The person can also retreat to a more
defensible position without specifically referencing the attack.
Politicians also use this strategy when you hear them say, "What
I really meant to say was. . . . " In contrast to the bolstering
strategy, all these defense strategies respond to specific attacks as
a means of maintaining ground in the battle. The bolstering moves
are more proactive in the sense that they try to build face regardless of what the other person does in the conflict.

(3) Face Attacking. Parties try to satisfy their face-saving needs
by portraying the other as incompetent or untrustworthy. In their
review, Wilson and Putnam (1990) found that people use attacks:
(1) to take the offense against other attacks; (2) to resist persuasive
appeals, particularly in the presence of influential others; (3) to
demand compliance with some relational obligation; or (4) to prod
the other into making concessions.

Extreme face attacks might also be viewed as verbal aggression: interaction-based attacks on one's situational identity, which consists of values central to that person, including honesty, integrity and commitment. As Felson's (1984) research indicates, such person-centered attacks often escalate out of control until either a third party cuts them off or there is violence.

(4) Face Supporting. The goal of face supporting is to bolster the other's image in some way to help that person fulfill his or her role obligations and protect role identities. For example, often after labor-management bargaining each side publicly tells the media that the other side was a tough opponent and concessions were difficult to obtain. By supporting the other side's face, each group can look good to its constituency.

Using these face-supporting tactics during bargaining might also encourage the other to make concessions or perhaps help to deescalate the verbal aggression cycle. In a study of the effects of face support, Tjosvold and Huston (1978) found that bargainers feel personally rejected when their opponents reject their demands without also supporting their face. If allowed to persist, such feelings could serve as the seeds for further attack and even verbal aggression down the line. So supporting the other's face reduces that person's need to attack.

Specific face-support efforts include face-honoring behaviors that give social support to the other (see Rogan, Donohue & Lyles, 1990) by trying to bolster the other's image (Table 3.2). For example, during divorce mediation the husband might use the following face-honoring tactic to build more cooperation into the interaction: "I think you're an excellent mother. You have a fine relationship with the children." Another kind of face-support tactic involves face-compensating behaviors. Perhaps the most common face-compensating tactic is the apology. It seeks to acknowledge wrong- doing while trying to compensate with such supportive comments as "I'm sorry for showing up late on Timmy's visitation the other day." The apology serves as the compensation for past transgressions and bolsters the other's image by admitting the other person was right all along.

Table 3.2 Assessing Your Actions to Support the Other's Face

The purpose of this questionnaire is to help you assess the kinds of strategies you prefer in supporting another's face in conflict. Respond to each statement by indicating the degree to which the statement is true for you.

If you "Never" take this action, answer 1;

if you "Almost Never" take this action, answer 2;

if you "Sometimes" take this action, answer 3;

if you "Almost Always" take this action, answer 4;

if you "Always" take this action, answer 5.

When I am in conflict with someone, I:

_____ try to make them look good.

_____ try to make them feel safe.

_____ try to make them believe I am honest.

_____ try to make them feel important.

_____ try to make them feel they are winning.

To find your score, add the numbers next to each item. Scores range from 5 to 25. The higher your score, the more effort you make in supporting the other's face and promoting a more cooperative interaction climate.

To illustrate the four face needs, examine the following sets of attributions given by two students. The first is a female student describing a fight with her boyfriend. She claimed that the fight occurred because, "He always says things that put me on the defensive." The causes of the conflict in her view include:

1. "He thinks I am a female with a bad attitude."
2. "I have strong opinions that I don't mind defending."
3. "He constantly questions everything I say."

In the second conflict, a male student identified the causes of a dispute with his girlfriend as including the following:

1. "She hates to be proven wrong."
2. "I, after winning, continued to talk about anything. I just babbled."

What kind of face needs are illustrated here? For the female student, it seems clear that she *maintains* her face in the relationship by having strong opinions about issues. The strong opinions seek to garner respect. She expresses displeasure at the notion that she has a "bad attitude," and is questioned constantly. Clearly, she needs to save face here.

The male student provides some interesting illustrations of face attack and support. In the first comment, he expresses his own need to attack his girlfriend's face to prove her wrong. However, once he believes that he accomplishes this task and wins the argument, he babbles. Perhaps his goal in babbling is to support her face by showing that he continues to respect her views and engage her in conversation. Perhaps he is *embarrassed* about winning.

❑ Attribution and Face: Recommendations for Action

THE INTERFACE

How do the ideas associated with attribution and face overlap? Actually, the concepts work together in conflict in a very interesting way. Basically, the kinds of attributions people form about conflict influence their face needs. Think about the relationship during the period of differentiation. Last week, two neighbors started a dispute about property rights, with one claiming the right to drive over the other's property. They began the dispute focusing on different views of their rights. One neighbor claimed right-of-way privileges and accused the other of being an unreasonable person. This type of comment clearly attacks the neighbor's need to be seen as a reasonable person who is just standing up for his rights. So one party's attribution stimulated the other's face need.

Consider the opposite situation in which the neighbors began the dispute by attributing the problem to their own behavior or lack of knowledge about property rights. Attribution theory predicts that this behavior would probably move parties into an integration phase, characterized by extensive information sharing and cooperative problem solving. This kind of cooperation might stimulate bolstering and supporting face needs as parties try to help each other. These examples suggest that the kind of attributions parties make stimulate a variety of face needs that can either enhance or hinder productive conflict management. The important concern is how to control attributions, and in so doing, control face needs to avoid too much danger in conflict.

CONTROLLING FACE THROUGH CONTROLLING ATTRIBUTIONS

The first step in controlling face problems is controlling our attributions. We need to make more self-attributions when examining our role in disputes. A major beneficiary of this move toward self-attributions is the relationship between the parties. By saying that we share blame for a problem commits us to share responsibility for correcting the problem together. The personality attribution says that others are responsible for *the entire* problem; therefore, they must do *all* the changing to resolve it. When people share the need to change, they make a commitment to work collaboratively and thus toward an improved relationship. So one of the first steps toward moving out of crisis is to look inward at your role in the conflict.

However, as you read these words, you are probably saying to yourself, "Hey, I'm not the one that usually starts the conflict. The other person always starts it, and I am just an innocent bystander." Notice that this comment is an external attribution and lays all the blame on the other person's doorstep. Your comment is also a face-saving device because you do not want to be seen as a troublemaker. Do you see how easy it is to make external attributions and how they quickly stimulate face needs?

Regardless of this little problem, assume for the moment that another person engages you in conflict that catches you by complete surprise. This is certainly not an unusual event for most people. You must deal with it on the spot. Unfortunately, you anticipate that this other person will attribute the problem to your personality traits and, in turn, threaten your face.

How do you prevent the conflict from escalating to a destructive spiral of relational issues? Attribution theory tells us that, first and foremost, we must not overreact and begin making only external attributions about the other's behavior. If we do, we will either threaten their face, thereby escalating the conflict, or simply give up and avoid the conflict. So our first strategy is to make the internal attribution and say, "Gee, maybe I should hear this person out to see if I am guilty of causing some problem."

In other words, using the active listening skills discussed in the last chapter would be valuable here. Asking questions, paying attention, showing involvement in the conversation, and repeating the other's comments demonstrates your sensitivity to the problem. This approach stimulates a valuable information-exchange process that works effectively in correcting false attributions. So if the other person attributes the cause of the problem to your insensitivity, respond with, "Tell me more," instead of, "That's because you are a bad listener." Avoid trying to kill one external attribution with another. It only stimulates more face problems.

A second way of heading off face problems that stem from external attributions comes from the empathy research reported in the last chapter. Recall that when we empathize, we reflect the person's feelings and ask for clarification. Because his or her ill feelings probably stem from the violation of a personal need, the other person will probably respond with an external attribution aimed at you—and it will probably threaten your face. However, when you grant the importance of the other's feelings, you reduce his or her defensiveness. All that person must do now is to focus on the problem, which is your ultimate goal. Part of this granting importance might involve self-disclosure about your own contributions to the problem. Such disclosure pressures the other person to assess his or her own role in the conflict.

To summarize, attributions about the other person's personality just stimulate face attacking and the defense of needs. We avoid these problems by rejecting our emotional desire to make such attributions and by exchanging information with the other party. Try to share personal information about your own role in the conflict. This strategy prevents the stimulation of face attacking and the defense of needs and places you in a position of functional problem solving.

TRAINED INCAPACITIES

Why is it so difficult for most of us to implement this strategy? Certainly, emotions spring forth to protect our personal needs, particularly our face. However, one other barrier impedes our ability to implement this strategy: *trained incapacities*. Folger and Poole (1984) use this concept to describe how behaviors that we find useful in managing our everyday lives can become useless, and even destructive, in managing a conflict. For example, remember the person who had trouble relating to his daughter because he tried to help her by using the same problem-solving approach he used at work? He learned to solve problems at work quickly without listening to people or being sensitive to their emotions. This training incapacitated him to deal with his daughter's problems. He thought it took too much time to reflect feelings, actively listen, and self-disclose. At work this approach may be successful, but in family crises, this approach is dead wrong.

What kind of trained incapacities have we picked up over the years that encourage us to make external attributions? One of the more interesting priorities of Western culture is its focus on the individual. Western countries hold individuals accountable for the performance of groups. Perhaps the best example is sports. In team sports such as football, fans focus on individual players even though these players' performances depend heavily on the other players on the field. The most commonly cited statistics focus on "skilled" players such as quarterbacks, running backs, and receivers. In business, government, education, and most other Western institutions, organizations have charts that list individuals' responsibilities and they hold them accountable for the organization's behavior.

In contrast, the Japanese are not individually oriented. They believe that the individual is subordinate to the group. Organizational charts never list individuals. They list teams of people and how the groups interact with one another. Japanese business leaders promote people based on their human relations qualities as opposed to their technical skills (Ouchi, 1981).

Does this focus on the individual encourage us to blame others when difficulties arise? Do we quickly look for explanations that center on the individual's personal qualities? The explosion of popular psychological literature in college courses, on television, and in the print media provides us with many labels for the behavior of others. We think we know all about such problems as aggressiveness, weak self-concepts, or various complexes people might display. Indeed, the conflict literature in many fields focuses on individual personality traits or particular behavioral styles to account for conflict behavior.

From this, we might draw the conclusion that the cultural focus on individuals and their psychological weaknesses can become a trained incapacity when we encounter conflict. Faced with a personally stressful situation, we search outward for the source of the problem as the most simple way of dealing with it. When we turn outward, we search for other individuals, and their problems, to blame for the conflict. At this point, the vicious circle begins, because when we make this external attribution we are more likely to avoid the conflict knowing, "You can't change people anyway." Even when others force us to confront the conflict, we often begin the process by making the external attributions that lead to face threats. This adds to the destructive potential of the interaction. The attribution stimulates face-protection needs, and thus the relational problems grow.

This chapter has tried to encourage you to skip this first impulse to focus on the other person's weaknesses and instead focus on your behavior and the problem at hand. That first impulse is another form of "getting stupid." Follow the recommendations to confront the problem as soon as possible, listen to the other person, focus on the problem, and take your time. These simple steps will help you keep away from external attributions, stimulate face-support needs, and help build productive problem solving. They are important steps to help you get smart in conflict.

Structuring the Issues

You now command many skills needed to focus your conflicts on issues and away from personalities. People grow angry when others attack their face or their personality. Steering people away from these personal needs promotes more productive conflict management. But once people can focus on the issues, what's next? How can you structure your discussion to keep the interaction focused and civil? Do you remember those structuring techniques used to avert a crisis? This chapter expands that discussion to more routine conflict situations. It describes how to create a discussion structure that keeps conflict moving along productively.

Let's review why structure promotes productive conflict. To illustrate how structure positively impacts conflict, consider a movie made several years ago called *Rollerball*, starring James Caan. It takes place in some futuristic society in which the government controls the population by allowing them to watch a game on television called Rollerball. The game is a cross between polo and roller-derby. The players chase a big steel ball around an indoor track on motorcycles. They score by capturing the ball and placing it in the opponent's goal (actually a hole in the wall). Scoring is difficult because players try to knock the other team off their motorcycles to keep them away from the rollerball. The game consists of many rules, much like football, in which players receive penalties for playing unfairly or too roughly.

In the movie, the government fears that James Caan, the best rollerball player, is growing too popular, thereby threatening government control. But the government cannot simply abolish the game, because people like it too much. So they decide to hold a final rollerball tournament and strip away most of the rules, hoping that all the players will kill each other. Of course, the lack of rules takes its toll. Players start killing each other to win, with the predictable outcome that they all die, except for James Caan. Because he is the only player left alive, he wins the game and, therefore, emerges more powerful than ever.

The point is that whenever parties fight without rules, they use whatever method necessary to gain an advantage. Rules constrain people. They equalize the conflict so people play fairly. They provide organization in the face of chaos. Of course, too many rules can choke off attempts to air concerns. Just the right number of rules keeps disputants in line and focused on the task.

Although the path is difficult, the direction is clear. Moving productively through conflict means walking the line between too much and too little structure. How do we do it? What kinds of conflict management procedures yield just the right amount of structure? This chapter now turns toward addressing this key issue.

❑ Phases in Conflict

Too much structure means too many rules for communicating. For example, labor-management negotiations in many industrial areas use rules that limit discussions to three topics: wages, hours, and working conditions. Any other kinds of discussions are off limits. If they want to work together to invent creative manufacturing procedures, the rules prevent them from doing so.

Think about the concept of too much structure in terms of common conversational habits. Do you recall the seven-word rule (speakers get seven words to express their thoughts, followed by a quick interruption and a new topic)? This habit creates too much structure. The rule limits flexibility. Do you have any conversational habits that limit someone else's ability to tell you how they feel? The key to working through conflict is to develop a structure that gives you some rules but also lets you express yourself flexibly. The goal is to limit potentially destructive communication while expanding potentially constructive communication.

How can you do it? Conflict management professionals set up conflict phases, or segments. They break the conflict into smaller pieces and focus on one piece at a time. Each establishes a target or goal that parties try to achieve. For example, in the first phase, *orientation*, parties try to learn more about the conflict management process. Once they complete the orientation and people feel comfortable with the process, they move to the next phase.

To understand the need to break down a conflict into smaller parts, consider the following interaction. This dialogue between a woman and her boyfriend deals with her sleeping over at his apartment.

WOMAN: I don't want to spend the night with someone who doesn't respect me.

MAN: I'm not just going to sit around and wait until it is convenient for you to come over to my apartment. I really like our time together.

WOMAN: [*in a sarcastic tone*] Okay, I'll come over tonight, if it will calm your insecurities.

MAN: Forget it! Tonight isn't convenient if you're going to run that crap on me!

This dialogue represents a classic multiple-issue problem. The couple struggles with the issues of respect, intimacy, insecurity, and privacy. And, like most couples, they try to talk about all these issues at once. Progress remains difficult with such ambitious goals. Perhaps they should try to tackle one issue at a time. To begin, the boyfriend might have probed the respect issue in his first comment.

He could ask several questions about his girlfriend's feelings on the respect issue to learn more about the problem. Instead, he vents his frustrations and ultimately moves to end the possibility of intimacy.

Breaking down the discussion into smaller parts keeps it manageable. That's what professional conflict managers do when they structure conflict into phases. They encourage parties to work toward one specific goal at a time. This process makes the conflict look much less threatening, and much more approachable.

Unfortunately, when people get upset and stop thinking (get stupid), they experience trouble sticking to a phase structure. They simply talk past each other and jump from issue to issue. It takes a great deal of discipline to implement a phase structure, particularly when the discussion focuses on needs-centered topics. People want to get even. They don't want to think about goals. Furthermore, people experience difficulty using phases because of the complexity of conflict itself. Thinking about your goals and how to accomplish them in phases is an overwhelming challenge. Can you imagine fighting with a friend and suddenly stopping the conversation to enforce some phase structure? Phases work best as a general guide in structuring your own thinking and planning about conflict.

For example, hostage negotiators face the difficult task of communicating with irrational hostage takers. The hostage takers switch topics constantly as they ramble on. They might begin with a set of demands and then talk about some intense personal problem. To deal with this unpredictability, police negotiators keep a general phase outline in their heads to decide where to go next. This outline helps them frame questions and determine their progress in freeing the hostages. Actually, the phase outline they use is very similar to the one provided below.

The point is that the phase outline works best as a general guideline or tool to break down, and get a handle on, your conflicts. Look at these phases as a flexible means of problem solving and not rigid prescriptions for action. Let's now define these phases and see how they work.

PHASE 1: SETTING THE STAGE

Your first move in a conflict is very important. Confronting the problem and getting people calmed down and ready to discuss the problem are difficult tasks. Phase 1 begins at the point at which people feel ready to sit down and discuss their problems.

Divorce mediation provides a good example of how this first phase works. In divorce mediation, neutral third parties help divorcing couples work out child custody and visitation arrangements. By the time divorcing couples enter mediation, most are ready to focus on these problems. They have already confronted the problems and expressed feelings about them and thus enter mediation ready to negotiate.

A key task involves setting the stage for discussion. The goal of this phase is orienting parties to the mediation process. In other words, parties need to establish a problem-solving frame of mind in several ways. First, they need to agree on some discussion rules. Common rules include no interrupting, be honest, and no bad mouthing the other party. Mediators know the importance of enforcing these rules, particularly during the first several minutes of interaction. These initial exchanges often become needs centered very quickly as parties vent their frustrations.

Second, mediators must reinforce the main objective of the mediation. In divorce mediation, the mediators tell couples to focus on building an agreement "in the best interests of the child." The child's welfare is the main reason to resolve a divorce cooperatively. Losing this focus encourages parents to turn on each other and become very destructive. As you can see, clarifying goals is critical to the success of the interaction.

Related to goals clarification is getting a commitment to negotiate. How much do parties really want to solve their problems? Many conflicts last forever because one or both parties want to make the conflict last, perhaps just to continue the relationship. If they want to use mediation to abuse each other, the session fails miserably. Have you ever heard people comment about their ex-spouse, "She (or he) won't let me go." One party may seek to terminate, while the other wants to continue the relationship. Inconsistent goals can quickly make a conflict destructive.

PHASE 2: DEFINING THE ISSUES

After establishing motivations and rules, the next step involves pulling out the key issues in dispute. This task is extremely difficult because it involves a great deal of listening. People must listen to one another's problems without turning hostile and defensive.

For example, what if your friend said that a key issue is, "You don't treat me with respect." Your natural tendency is to jump up and cry, "I do so!" This defensive reaction will probably escalate the expression of concern, because the other person senses that you are not listening. Avoid these kinds of defensive reactions. People are angry and need to express key problems. Glossing over the problem only makes things worse. Or when the other person expresses a problem, it is also counterproductive to jump in immediately with a solution. Have you ever reacted to someone's concern about your behavior with some comment like, "Well, I just won't do that anymore, if that will make you happy"? Such snap decisions about solutions are premature. Remember, the other person is venting and needs your full attention so you can understand exactly what the key issues are that led to the problem.

The trick to drawing out issues is probing for the *real* issue. In many cases, people articulate surface problems and avoid the real one. These are really "toilet seat" disputes. Have you ever heard of couples fighting about leaving the toilet seat up? The real issue is not the toilet seat position, but showing a lack of respect for the other's desires. Or the problem might involve a fundamental relational or value problem. People fight about the toilet seat to avoid the deeper issue. The conflict will never go away as long as the more important issues remain.

To illustrate, consider the conflict at the beginning of this chapter. The real issue was not spending the night. Those interests started the discussion; yet, it quickly escalated into a needs-violation problem. The woman accused her boyfriend of not respecting her. The man countered with an issue of wanting more intimacy in the relationship. The woman followed with a personality attribution about her boyfriend's insecurities. He ended the argument with a face-saving strategy.

What is the most critical issue in this conflict? Is it staying over-night, respect, or intimacy? Clearly, the most critical issue is the woman's personal need for respect. The negotiation goes no further until the man grants her need for respect in the relationship. Staying over is secondary and hides the true issue. Respect is also a big barrier to the boyfriend's plea for increased intimacy. By not focusing on that issue, the argument will likely become destructive to the relationship.

When these kinds of discussions arise, how do you locate these more important issues? Look first at the intensity of the discussion. If the discussion looks heated, then it indicates possible needs violations. Look second at whether or not people keep repeating themselves. Until the other grants the individual's personal needs, the individual will bring up the issue repeatedly as a means of asking the other to grant the personal needs. Think of the last time you kept repeating a problem to someone. The problem reflected your desire for the other to listen to you or to respect your opinions. Thus, intense language and issue repetition are good signs that deeper issues beg for discussion.

One of the best practical ways of discussing key issues is to use newsprint, or a big flip chart. Go through one issue at a time. Write each problem down, regardless of its content, and do it until all the issues appear on the chart. This gives you the big picture of what the conflict entails. Again, this step is difficult because most people want to discuss each issue as it arises. Resist that temptation and wait for all issues to surface. The effect of placing all these issues on paper gives people the sense that they can manage the conflict. When people bring the issues out in the open, they can see the whole problem in black and white. The impossible dream of resolving the dispute suddenly seems possible.

PHASE 3: PROCESSING THE ISSUES

At this point you should have a list of all the issues that separate the parties. Now comes the job of working through them. Ideally, experienced conflict managers like to start by prioritizing issues from least to most controversial. Prioritizing allows parties to start talking about the least controversial issues first, so they can develop a working relationship during the conflict. They need some successes before moving into the really tough issues.

Hostage negotiators also use this principle. Hostage takers often begin with a series of demands that they want filled "right now!" The police negotiator picks the easy ones first, like food or media attention, to start the bargaining process. Once they get to know each other, they can discuss the more difficult demands.

However, many times people insist on discussing the difficult problems first. When they make these demands, try a delaying tactic. A common delaying tactic includes assuring the person that the issue will be discussed in time. If this fails to satisfy the person, then discuss the tough issue first. Of course, the good news is that if you resolve that issue, every other issue is that much easier to address.

What other criteria should you use to decide the order in which issues will be discussed? Consider the type of issue when deciding the discussion order. Most conflict professionals recognize at least five types of issues:

1. *Data or factual issues.* These issues examine whether something is true or false, e.g., what time your roommate came home from the party.
2. *Interest issues.* These issues deal with what the parties want to achieve, e.g., "I want more money at my workplace".
3. *Relational and power issues.* These issues include people's feelings about each other and their rights in directing the relationship, e.g., whether or not a co-worker has the right to order you to do something.
4. *Value issues.* These issues are related to whether or not something is right or wrong, good or bad, e.g., freedom-of-speech controversies involving core values.
5. *Emotional issues.* These issues are tied to an individual's personal needs, e.g., fairness, respect, and dignity.

In your experience, which of these five issues is easiest to deal with? Perhaps the factual issues are easiest because they can be resolved with objective evidence. On the other hand, the emotional issues can be the most difficult because they are so personally involving. They threaten individual needs and can produce

Table 4.1 Assessing Your Ability to Categorize Issues

To illustrate the difference between the five types of issues, consider the following interaction between a manager and a restaurant server. As you read, try to categorize each person's comments into the five types of issues:

D for data or factual,

I for interest,

R for relational,

V for value, and

E for emotional

_____Manager: You came to work late again today.

_____Server: You never talk to your girlfriend, Liz, when she's late. If you're going to clamp down on me, clamp down on everybody.

_____Manager: This is between you and me. You clean up your act and stop partying so much so you can get to work on time.

_____Server: What gives you the right to tell me how to run my life?

_____Manager: I believe that living clean is necessary to get ahead in life, that's all.

_____Server: Look, all I want from this place is some money for school.

Did you categorize the statements? The first comment by the manager seeks to promote a factual dispute about when the server came to work. The server's response is an emotional reaction around the topic of being treated fairly. The third and fourth comments represent a relational/ power dispute over rights and responsibilities. The manager's next comment expresses a value about clean living, and the final comment by the server expresses an interest in receiving a paycheck. So the right answers are D, E, R, R, V, and I.

---

very intense reactions. Certainly, challenging someone's power and authority and their value systems also stirs a great deal of controversy (Table 4.1).

The best advice is to focus on the factual and interest issues first and to see if some agreement can be reached there. But what if people are so emotionally involved that they are unwilling to bargain? Again, this chapter assumes that you are past that point, and the emotional issues no longer threaten the discussion's progress. In general, try to work on the facts and interests first and keep the values discussions until later.

After parties pick an issue and begin the discussion, what should they talk about first? Begin with gathering objective information: who is involved, what is each person's current situation, and how important is the issue? Allow plenty of time for this information search so parties can build a working relationship. Hostage negotiators and divorce mediators thoroughly believe in gathering background information first because it forms a working relationship. They start talking about uncontroversial information just to get started.

Once the background information is gathered, what general strategies can parties use to approach each kind of issue? Some guidelines are helpful, because each issue type requires a different approach. Consider these guidelines for each type of issue:

(1) Data or Factual Conflicts. The main problem is trying to agree on what information will be used to resolve the factual dispute. For example, many labor-management disputes often deal with whether or not certain pay scales are comparable to workers in similar industries. The conflict revolves around defining which similar industries to include in the comparison list. The general approach to these disputes involves developing criteria for what information will be included for consideration.

(2) Interest Conflicts. The main processing challenge involves identifying what people really want. In many conflicts, people may identify one objective by asking for something completely different. For example, when couples divorce, they often make very harsh demands for things they really don't want. They use the demands to punish the other person for some problem that happened in the past. Parties can sort out this confusion by carefully probing the other's position statements. Do the individuals really want what they say they want? Never accept initial positions on face value. Probe more deeply and try to expose each person's underlying interests.

(3) Relational and Power Issues. Relational and power issues start to present some real processing challenges, because of their personal nature. Above all, respect these problems, because relationships and power represent very sensitive topics. Issues of intimacy, trust, and control represent three of the most difficult topics that people must address. Parties must exercise great care in how and when they discuss these issues. You probably know when these

> *The first key to processing relational and power issues is to keep them centered on substance.*

issues arise, because people often express them using intense language such as swearing or big words.

Should you encourage people to use this kind of intense language? In general, it shows involvement and interest in the problem. As long as the intensity insults or harms no one, consider allowing it. Intense language reveals feelings. When you understand feelings, you gain great insights into the issues.

This discussion suggests that the first key to processing relational and power issues is to keep them centered on substance. Is that difficult when one party has more power than the other party? Divorce mediators face that problem all the time. Frequently, husbands enter mediation with more financial resources than wives (Weitzman, 1985). Or one party might have better communication skills and thus intimidate the other. When these problems occur, use some of the power-balancing strategies outlined in Chapter 5. Parties need to interact on an equal footing for conflict to work out constructively.

In practical terms, when you see power or relationship issues, ask the parties to identify them. They probably can't see these issues very clearly. When they finally recognize such issues, they can begin to see how they impede constructive conflict. They can also identify their behaviors linked to these power and relationship problems. Perhaps the person interrupts too often and the other interprets it as a power move. Ask how each can change their behaviors to overcome relational misunderstandings. If you provide such insights, you have done a great deal.

(4) Value Issues. As indicated earlier, value conflicts are tricky. The general processing strategy involves two approaches. First, each side needs to identify the value at the core of the dispute. One side might believe one value is at stake while the other might see another value as the core problem. If you cannot agree on the value in dispute, destructive conflict may result. Can value conflicts be resolved? Value conflicts do not lend themselves to integrative solutions, because most people remain inflexible about their values.

The approach here is simply to respect one another's values and find some other way out of the conflict. Leas and Kittlaus (1973) contend that most individuals have values that are simply not negotiable. Indeed, the only real option is to identify the issue and agree to respect the other's position. The current abortion controversy in the United States is a value issue that continues to defy any compromise.

What other ways can you use to redirect a value conflict? One way involves translating the value conflict into an interest conflict. For example, have you ever fought with someone about their dating values? One person might value punctuality, whereas the other holds no value for it at all. Both sides can respect the other's values by translating the value issue into an interest issue. In this case, the parties might agree to keep each other informed about being late for a date. The parties retain their values, but their behaviors change to accommodate the other's interests.

(5) Emotional Issues. Emotional conflicts look a lot like power, relational, and sometimes value conflicts. The key differentiating element is self-concept. If the issue really is aimed at hurting the person's self-image, it is an emotional conflict. Such issues may be confused with other conflicts, because people use intense language to express themselves. The best strategy for first confronting such people is to *listen.* Allow the other person to vent and try to be supportive and, perhaps, empathic. Be open to criticism and avoid showing resistance.

In terms of processing emotional issues, the principal objective is to learn about the problem. The parties involved probably cannot see the emotional issue. Identifying it and asking for background information about the problem helps to move parties toward problem solving. Once you learn about the problem, then you can propose changing specific behaviors that cause the emotional problem. Some might involve simple adjustments in, for example, conversational habits like taking turns and not interrupting. Other behavior changes may prove more difficult, requiring more complex interventions. But look for the simple changes first.

PHASE 4: RESOLVING THE ISSUES

Once parties identify important issues and discuss them carefully, they can begin creating options to solve the problem. What does each side want to do to address the issues? The real success of this phase comes from developing many options, each of which receives careful attention. For example, each side might generate two or three workable solutions based on their perspectives of the issues.

To illustrate, consider the following problem. Suppose a husband asks his wife if he can manage the family checkbook, which has been her responsibility for several years. First of all, what kind of issue surfaces in this request? Is it a power issue or a simple interest issue? As the couple discusses the switch, they need to address these questions. If the husband wants more power in the relationship but the wife wants to retain her control of the money, they should address that issue directly. However, if the husband only wants to help out and contribute more to the family, it becomes an interest issue.

After discussing the switch thoroughly and deciding that the issue focuses on interests and not power, the parties can begin creating proposals for satisfying their interests. The husband might propose some kind of rotating system in which he paid the bills for one year on a trial basis. Then she could pay them the next year. She might modify the proposal to every six months and propose that he work with only regular, monthly bills. Whatever the solution they ultimately hammer out, the important feature of the discussion is the process. They sorted out the issues, moved to proposals, and then worked out a solution.

Once parties move to the proposal stage, they officially pass the point of differentiation and move into a period of integration. Parties stop focusing on differences and look toward their common concerns. They try to steer clear of the past and look toward the future. Remember, the goal is to move the discussion away from personalities and toward the external problem or interest that is dividing the parties.

However, be careful not to short-circuit this process. Many people make the mistake of moving too quickly into integration. Starting with proposals may not work because you will probably start with extreme proposals that irritate the other person. Remember, conflict involves emotions. When emotional, you may not control the quality of your contributions. You may make an extreme proposal that emphasizes differences, thereby discouraging parties from continuing.

> *Remember, time and communication are the most important enemies of destructive conflict.*

The key is patience. Remember, time and communication are the most important enemies of destructive conflict. As long as you keep talking by *listening* and *sharing*, you commit to making an integrative agreement, even though you find that process painful.

I hope that you get the point that integrative strategies require lots of time, trust, and openness in sharing information. When you hide information and try to rush through the conflict, you cut off creativity. Slowing down the conflict gives people time to think and, more important, time to learn to trust one another. The more time you build into the problem-solving process, the more time you have to develop trust. Hurrying the process only forces sides to focus on differences and not shared concerns.

Furthermore, integrative strategies work best when people are communicatively competent. Recall the discussion about collaboration. People collaborate best when they possess the communicative resources to argue for their position, share ideas, and develop options for solving their problems. Integrative strategies are the general means people use when they wish to be collaborative.

Perhaps integration asks too much from people. After all, most conflicts don't look very integrative; they look more like differentiation, and for good reason. When people enter conflict, they can only see the differences. Asking people to share information, prolong the conflict, trust one another, and communicate effectively is unrealistic. However, you must understand that integration is generally where people end up, and not where they start. When people work through their difficulties, they generally end up using integrative communication.

The validation communication sequence discussed in Chapter 2 is a classic example of this process. The couple begins with a set of concerns, but then ultimately comes around to using integrative tactics such as information sharing and showing support for the other's position. The point is to *be patient*. Integration can arrive if couples take their time and stick with the fight, that is, they avoid getting stupid.

When people pursue integrative strategies, what kind of face needs seem to follow? Unlike differentiation, integration stimulates needs for face support. People need to support each other when integrating. They need to see the conflict from the other person's perspective and help the other person be strong. When both people are strong, they have that much more energy to help each other. A second face need probably revolves around bolstering. Bolstering involves information sharing to make positions stronger. Any collaborative interaction demonstrates a great deal of these bolstering moves.

As you might expect, the hallmark of integrating is demonstrating flexibility about *methods* for achieving joint goals. Individuals can stick to their goals concerning *outcomes*, but when they show flexibility in how they reach those outcomes, they indicate a desire to be integrative. This demonstration sends a fairly important message. It says that the relationship that the parties share commands as much, if not more, importance than the outcome of the conflict. Integrating means strengthening the relationship, as suggested by the collaboration style of conflict. This point cannot be overemphasized. *The best way to achieve a satisfying, long-term working relationship involves a mutual commitment to helping each other solve problems.*

One of the best places to test your new integrative potential is in the actual agreements parties construct. The final issue about integration is *details*. When parties finally build their agreement, they need to tie up all the loose ends. Agreements need to be specific and objective. In divorce mediation, couples can agree in principle to an integrative custody arrangement, but it must be written and the parties must sign off on the arrangement. Clear and specific details help parties understand the agreements very thoroughly. Ambiguity leaves room for mistrust and escalation of the conflict to relational and emotional issues. Make the agreement specific to avoid future problems.

Many parties fail at this agreement-making process because they become impatient. They spent so much time getting to this stage that they want to be done with the conflict and thus lose interest in the details. This happens frequently in the U.S. Congress; legislators work hard to settle conflicts about particular bills but then leave loopholes in the legislation that finally becomes law.

Does this stuff really work? Does moving people systematically through these phases really make a difference? Studies in decision making in international crises explores the effects of planning and systematic problem solving on productive conflict management.

❑ Decision Making During International Crises

Over the past several years, social scientist Irving Janis and his colleagues have been working on a line of research to determine if systematic problem solving works better than simply winging it. When people take their time and, for example, work through the phases, does it pay off? In several books and articles (e.g., Janis, 1989; Herek, Janis, & Huth, 1989), they describe the concept of *vigilant problem solving*. What they contend is that successful decision making, really in any context, requires that the people remain vigilant. Decision makers must actively research the prob-

Table 4.2 Assessing Your Vigilant Problem-Solving Potential

The purpose of this questionnaire is to help you assess your ability to remain vigilant in a crisis situation. Respond to each statement by indicating the degree to which the statement is true for you.

If you "Never" take this action, answer 1;

if you "Almost Never" take this action, answer 2;

if you "Sometimes" take this action, answer 3;

if you "Almost Always" take this action, answer 4;

if you "Always" take this action, answer 5.

When I am in a crisis, I:

_____ try to consider *all* of the alternatives.

_____ try to consider the risks involved.

_____ try to make sure I gather all the facts.

_____ try to agree on times to negotiate.

_____ try to work out a detailed agreement.

To find your score, add the number you wrote next to each item. Scores range from 5 to 25. The higher your score, the more information you tend to gather when in a crisis.

lem and constantly stay alert to new information (Table 4.2). Why is information gathering in a crisis important? From their research, Janis and his colleagues found that groups make ineffective decisions when they make the following decision-making errors.

GROSS OMISSIONS IN SURVEYING ALTERNATIVES

The group fails to consider a wide range of workable, alternative policies. These groups concentrate their decision-making activities entirely on the course of action they preferred in the first place. So they confine their discussions to only one solution. You can easily understand why some groups make these omissions. People become emotionally attached to one solution and defend it at all costs.

For example, when most people turn 16, they want a car. Never mind that they do not need a car or cannot afford one. Teenagers focus exclusively on that objective and typically fight with their parents about it. Parents often see the issue as transportation. The teens see the issue as freedom and prestige. As a result, the parties run the danger of coming into the dispute with only one possible outcome on their mind. The parents will only accept the teen using the family wagon, and the teen will only accept a hot car of his or her own. When the parties persist in this focus on only their own solution, they confine their discussions to only that option. Narrow options do not provide much flexibility and integrative problem-solving potential.

GROSS OMISSIONS IN SURVEYING OBJECTIVES

The group never explicitly discusses objectives. What is the group trying to achieve in the conflict? Many groups lose sight of any meaningful objectives the more the conflict drags on. People become possessed with winning and forget about meaningful objectives. What are the major goals that each side wants to achieve? Losing sight of goals makes integrative problem solving very difficult. As a result, the lesson is clear. Never lose sight of your goals and, most important, the values implied by those goals. Groups that succeed constantly assess their goals and values and modify them when necessary.

FAILURE TO EXAMINE MAJOR COSTS AND RISKS OF THE PREFERRED CHOICE

The group fails to consider the costs associated with their preferred alternative. They typically think only about the positive results. However, all options involve costs if the decision turns out to be the wrong one. Consider the arms-for-hostages scandal during the Reagan administration. When it tried to sell weapons to Iran in exchange for the American hostages held in Lebanon, did the administration consider the costs of failure? When Saddam Hussein invaded Kuwait, did he anticipate that the world would support a boycott of Iraq? Perhaps he anticipated these costs.

However, failure to assess costs in the event of failure can yield unfortunate consequences. Groups often overlook these consequences even when information about those consequences is available.

POOR INFORMATION SEARCH

The group fails to obtain available information necessary for critically evaluating the pros and cons of the preferred course of action and other alternatives. The information is readily available, but the group simply ignores it. This selective information search supports biases, and even reinforces them. Even worse, the group shows a definite tendency to accept new information from experts, the mass media, and outside critics only when it supports the preferred alternative. As a result, the members generally ignore or refute many important pieces of nonsupporting information they encounter.

FAILURE TO RECONSIDER
ORIGINALLY REJECTED ALTERNATIVES

Failure to reconsider alternatives is common among decision makers. For most groups, once they reject some alternatives for solving the problem they ignore them, even in the face of new information about the problem. Or they might introduce bias into the process by discounting favorable information and believing only unfavorable information about the rejected alternatives. The group goes out of its way to bias its information search to support the preferred alternative. A simple example of buying a car illustrates this point. When you reject several alternative cars do you come back to them once you decide on the car you want? Most people do not reexamine the rejected cars, even when they learn about the preferred car's poor repair record.

FAILURE TO WORK OUT DETAILED IMPLEMENTATION,
MONITORING, AND CONTINGENCY PLANS

Often groups get so elated after reaching a basic agreement that they forget to work out the details of the agreement. Remember that parties must pay attention to those details, because they can make or break an agreement. They must specify agreement features so everyone understands the exact requirements of the agreement. Furthermore, problems in implementation might arise, which the group should consider and try to anticipate. Monitoring the agreement to see if problems arise is always a good strategy; it paves the way for prompt corrective action.

For your own benefit, consider a really difficult conflict you experienced recently that escalated into a crisis. Did you try vigilant problem solving in dealing with it? If not, how could you have approached the conflict had you used vigilant problem-solving techniques? Perhaps you would not have rushed into the dispute with only one solution. Maybe you would have created a variety of solutions and considered them carefully. Perhaps you might have considered more information that was not consistent with your preferred solution. The evidence suggests that this problem-solving technique works. Based on this knowledge, consider the following recommendations about problem solving.

❏ Recommendations About Structuring the Issues

Our discussions about phases, issues, and vigilant problem solving revolve around one simple principle: Structure works in conflict. People need rules to fight by. These simple recommendations might help sort out some of the ideas presented in this chapter.

PLANNING

When people move into conflict it is often spontaneous and not at all planned. Although planning is necessary, particularly with difficult conflicts, you might be able to manage the easy conflicts without planning. But remember, the difficult conflicts require some forethought.

PATIENCE

Take your time when fighting. You are much more likely to avoid getting stupid and starting a destructive cycle when you take your time. Slow down, build a structure, and then move through it slowly. Even if you lose your patience and walk out, try to come back and start again. Remember, running away can make matters much worse in the long term.

INFORMATION QUALITY

Try not to limit yourself to just a few pieces of information that simply support your point of view. Gather as much information as possible, and always remain open to new ideas.

UNDERLYING ISSUES

Many times, the issues people fight about are not the real issues dividing them. Analyze any of your recent conflicts. What were they really all about? Think about them. In all likelihood, some kind of relational, power, or emotional problem lurked around at the root of the dispute. Probe for these issues. Again, when you slow down the conflict, you give yourself the time to find these issues.

OPTIONS

Proposed solutions give people plenty of psychological space. What is psychological space? When people have no options they feel backed into a corner. When offered many options, we feel that the other person cares about protecting our rights. Expand your options and watch the creativity flow.

AGREEMENTS

If you lose the details, you may lose the opportunity for productive problem solving. Details make proposals work, so don't forget them.

In this chapter, you learned about productive problem solving in a general sense. Now you can learn more about the specifics of negotiation. Research in this area expands daily. In particular, scholars and practitioners are beginning to understand communication's important role in negotiation. So if you are interesting in sharpening your negotiation skills, read on.

5

Effective Negotiation

We learn negotiation skills at a very young age because we soon discover that getting what we want requires give and take. We ask for things, but we meet resistance in our requests. Coping with the resistance means learning to negotiate. Do you remember your first negotiation experience? Perhaps you once bargained with your parents about how many beans you had to eat in order to get dessert. You may recall negotiating with friends over prized toys or bubble gum. And, as you grew older, you enhanced your negotiation skills to cope with school, jobs, and intimate relationships.

Of course, "real" negotiation only becomes an option for resolving disputes after parties have addressed their relational and value disputes. Real negotiation involves the good faith exchange of proposals, counterproposals, and concessions to create agreements about some specific issue. Sometimes people use the word *negotiation* to describe any conflict, regardless of parties' intentions. All conflict is not necessarily good-faith negotiation. Negotiating in good faith means that parties sincerely want to work through the important issues dividing them. When parties try to negotiate without first resolving important relational difficulties, the interaction can degenerate quickly into name calling or worse.

For example, picture a negotiation session between divorced parents trying to create a visitation arrangement for their child. The father, who does not want the divorce, keeps throwing up roadblocks to serious negotiation. These negotiation sessions are his only contact with his ex-wife, so he wants to prolong them as much as possible. She wants to terminate the meetings quickly and focus on the task of arranging the visitation schedules. In this instance, the father is not negotiating in good faith but the mother, who wants to create an agreement, is. The couple's relational difficulties prevent this kind of progress. After parties work through their relational problems, negotiations can focus on the substantive issues separating parties.

Chapter 4 ended with six recommendations to help you work through sensitive relational and value issues and focus on the substantive problems. This chapter assumes that you have accomplished that goal. This is a big assumption, because the most difficult part of many negotiations is simply getting to the point at which parties are ready to exchange proposals in good faith. Now, assume you have done that and you are ready to learn how to negotiate.

Chapters 5 and 6 provide you with an overview of effective negotiation techniques. Chapter 5 focuses on power because power issues underlie negotiation strategies and tactics. Chapter 6 concentrates more on specific strategies and tactics and provides you with the practical skills needed to negotiate effectively. With that division in mind, it is time to turn the focus to social power.

❏ The Role of Power in Conflict

Any skilled negotiator understands the need to cast his or her strategies in the context of the disputant's power relationship. In any negotiation episode, either personal or international in scope, power balances or imbalances weigh heavily in understanding negotiation strategies and tactics. To fully comprehend this process, let's explore the basic principles of social power to see its structures and functions.

A RELATIONAL CONCEPT

Once a conflict emerges from the shadows of people's thoughts into an acknowledged dispute, parties assess their own resources to accomplish their goals in the con-

> *Power only makes sense in the context of the relationship between parties.*

flict. "What can I do to make the other person give in?" you might ask. If the conflict quickly settles into a focus on the issues, you begin to apprise the other person about the advantages of your position. You might also offer a tangible reward for complying. Or if desperation sets in, you might consider threats to withdraw a prized possession or opportunity if the other fails to comply with your demands.

This example suggests that we can define power as *the ability to influence or control events*. When one party can control or manipulate the other's behavior, or the circumstances surrounding that behavior, then that party, in that context, holds some degree of social power. Certainly, the more control exerted, the more power we believe that person possesses. However, power is not an individual concept; it is a relational concept. People do not possess power in the absence of other people. Power only makes sense in the context of the relationship between parties.

For example, how much power does any leader possess if that leader has no followers? How much power does a boss possess if the boss has no employees? Leaders and bosses only possess as much power as the followers or workers are willing to give them. If the followers decide that the leader can no longer exercise leadership skills, they stop following orders. This strips the leader of power. Presidents elected by a wide majority possess great power because many people expressed a desire to follow them. Presidents elected by slim majorities wield less power because fewer people expressed a willingness to follow them.

Can you think of anyone in your life that exercises great power over you? If so, their power derives from your willingness to give them power. If you walked away, or in other ways decreased their control over you, they would no longer posses power over you.

From this relational perspective, power really comes down to a dependency issue. The more people try to control one another, the more they confirm their interdependency. A couple that is very much in love controls each other's lives. People that love their leaders depend on those leaders for guidance. Love and dependency give those leaders tremendous control over their followers. Think about power and dependency in your own relationships. If you care what your friend thinks about you, then your friend possesses some power in the relationship.

What happens to power when relationships change? Power also changes, largely because dependencies change. Suppose a husband wants a divorce, but the wife wants to continue the marriage: Who holds greater power in this relationship? The pending divorce changes dependencies, so power must also change. In this situation, the husband holds greater power over the wife. She wants to be dependent on him, whereas he wants to be free from her. This point is important for negotiation because negotiators try to influence outcomes by manipulating dependencies. A union bargainer might try to gain power by demonstrating how dependent management is on the union. The union might strike or conduct other activities to demonstrate management's need to have them around.

AN ABSTRACT CONCEPT

Power shifts because dependencies shift. People change their feelings and perceptions of one another, sometimes from moment to moment. When feelings change, dependencies change. This creates a difficult problem in assessing how much power an individual possesses in a relationship. No standard measure of power is possible in such a changing context. As a result, power remains a very abstract concept. Negotiators consistently try to estimate or guess power levels of parties to judge parties' control over outcomes.

Negotiators use two general guidelines to assess power. First, does the individual appear to have the *ability* or resources to influence events? Second, does the person possess the *willingness* to use those resources? For example, consider the 1991 war in the Persian Gulf. Forces opposing the Allies wondered how much power the Allies had to influence events in the region. First, the leaders looked at Allied resources. Do they possess the military capability in the area to influence events? Second, are they willing to use those resources? If the answer is yes to both questions, then forces opposing the Allies *perceive* Allied power as being very high. Perception is important here because parties never really know the actual strength of an opponent. They can only *estimate* strength in terms of the ability and willingness variables. However, if the answers are yes to resources but no to willingness, then parties weaken their power. The Allies might be strong, but if the opponents perceive that the Allies lack the will to use their strength, their power decreases. Often negotiators try to create the perception that they have both the resources and the willingness to use them. They hope this abstract impression of strength might encourage the opponent to concede or develop more flexible demands.

What happens when people actually use their power? The most interesting effect is that power moves from an abstract impression to a concrete event. The willingness to use power becomes concrete along with the resources and the use of power commands. For example, when nations start wars they show a willingness to fight while also showing the enemy what kinds of weapons and other resources they control. So, in a sense, using power reveals the user's cards and makes power less of a mythical, abstract concept.

What is the effect of this transformation? A primary effect is frequently the erosion of power. When power is abstract, the low-power party is more hesitant to challenge the other's power. The abstract nature of the other's power renders the situation uncertain, making it difficult to predict what might happen after the challenge.

However, when power becomes concrete, the parties learn quickly what they face and how to counteract the other's power. You might learn that the other party commands fewer resources than you suspected. You also develop some reference points to determine how best to counter the power move. Thus power is often greater in its abstract form than in its concrete form. Once used, it becomes understood and, therefore, less psychologically threatening. Negotiators are aware of this power principle, so they try to avoid direct power use when possible.

In some circumstances, using power enhances the individual's ability to control resources, particularly when the other party believes that the individual lacks the will to use power. Again, by showing a willingness to use it, power increases. The main lesson here is that power flows in elusive ways that remain difficult to estimate. The art of politics and negotiation involves estimating power and how it changes from moment to moment.

❑ Levels of Dependency

This discussion will reveal that understanding power comes down to understanding how people manipulate dependencies. In what social areas do people become dependent on one another? In other words, how do they connect with one another socially? Understanding these social connections is very important because negotiators manipulate connections for their advantage. For example, did you ever notice at work how some people appear very friendly and informal when they want something from you? They are drawing on their personal connection with you as a persuasive device. You may want to keep the relationship at a formal level to remind the person that the discussion is all business. However, the other person wants to communicate at a more personal level to increase his or her leverage. That manipulation attempt is a kind of mininegotiation. One person wants to define the relationship one way, whereas the other wants a different definition of the relationship.

So what are some of the other social connections, or types of social dependencies, that people draw on during conflict and negotiation? Five types are important here, and they range from a very broad and abstract level to a very narrow and specific level.

They include culture, ideology, institution, relationship, and language. Let's look at each in detail.

CULTURE

Culture consists of people's values about what is good and bad in a society. These values often translate into customs and rituals of all types. We rely heavily on customs when we meet people socially. Do you hold doors for women if you are male? Do you expect to go through a door first if you are female? Culture guides our beliefs about the right and wrong ways to treat people. In some Asian cultures, people believe that it is wrong to disagree openly with others, because it communicates lack of respect for that person. Also, people in these same cultures believe that developing trust must be established before business can be conducted.

What happens when people from different cultures conflict? Each party wants to impose its own culture on the other party. For example, when Americans first began negotiating with the Japanese in Japan, they became very frustrated. The Americans would fly over to Japan for a two-week stay, expecting to talk business right away. In contrast, the Japanese delayed any business talk until they developed a relationship with the Americans, because they believe that trust must be established before business can be conducted. This frustrated the Americans as they repeatedly tried to talk business because their trip time was running out. Finally, near the end of the visit, the Japanese would talk business and have the upper hand because, by that time, the Americans were willing to settle for anything. In this example, each side sought to make the other dependent on its respective culture. The negotiation was really about culture and not business.

IDEOLOGY

An individual's ideology consists of that person's beliefs about social order. What is true and false about an individual's place in society? Do you believe that all people should have equal rights or do you believe that some people are more entitled to some rights than others? For example, in many parts of the world children (defined by a certain age) possess fewer rights than adults. In the United States, adults—but not children—can legally consume alcohol, vote, own property, enter contests, and become contestants on game shows. However, in other parts of the world, children have nearly the same rights as adults. Our ideology tells us where people belong in the social order.

Many conflicts deal primarily with ideology. Teens often protest to their parents that they should have more rights of self-determination. Parents, on the other hand, may cling to an ideology that teens are not capable of judging right and wrong for themselves. The teens try to impose an egalitarian (all people are equal) perspective on the parents, whereas the parents seek to impose a more traditional ideology on the teens. Many conflicts addressing race, gender, or age really stem from issues of ideology, or beliefs about the social order. One side seeks to impose its beliefs on the other.

INSTITUTION

When people work together in groups for sustained periods of time, they create institutions. Institutions are organizations that have unique social environments. People grow interdependent in organizations and create their own unique organizational habits. These habits turn into norms, or standard ways of behaving. You might think of such habits as "the ropes," or what people must know to be successful in an organization.

Most people think of an organization as their place of employment. But examples of institutions include government bureaus, fraternities and sororities, and even families. In fact, the first organization most people come to understand is their family. We learn fairly quickly that organizations expect us to behave in certain ways. Perhaps your family required proper table manners and scolded you for holding your fork wrong or chewing food with your mouth open. Maybe you needed to talk very quickly in your house because others interrupted you frequently. Or you might have had rules in your family about how to address relatives, request favors from your parents, and discuss family business with the neighbors.

These do's and don'ts, most of which are very informal, structure our communication habits in every organization to which we belong. We become accustomed to communicating in particular ways, largely because they work for us. These habits, or conventions, are comfortable and functional for getting the job done. Naturally, we wish to use these habits and conventions when negotiating. We want people to abide by our rules because we like them and they work for us.

For example, labor-management negotiations in the 1990s have experienced some radical changes due to differences in institutional norms. Many industries currently use team-based manufacturing methods in which labor and management work side by side. Using this approach, they informally decide production policies cooperatively. What would happen to such a company if it were taken over by a corporation accustomed to a more authoritarian decision-making system? The workers would probably resist such a move, because they enjoyed much more flexible institutional norms.

When negotiators try to impose their institutional norms on another, they access institutional power. Police frequently try to impose their norms on hostage takers in hostage negotiation situations. They try to take a rational approach to problem solving in a manner that is consistent with the way police do their business. The hostage takers often resist these attempts to structure their problem-solving methods by acting more irrationally toward the police. Accepting the other's norms submits to the other's power.

RELATIONSHIP

When people develop an important friendship, they build a set of behavior patterns that are unique to that dyad, or couple. This unique set of patterns can be termed a *personal relationship*. In personal relationships, people ultimately must work through three important issues:

1. *Control.* Control deals with dominance issues. Does one person call the shots or is control over the meaning and direction of the relationship shared equally?
2. *Trust.* Trust brings forth the issue of exploitation. Does each person believe that the other will not exploit or abuse their relationship in any way?
3. *Intimacy.* Intimacy addresses the issue of feelings. Are the parties personally attracted to one another?

Every relationship demands that couples negotiate these three issues. The negotiation typically takes the form of subtle give and take. Rarely do couples come right out and make demands on these issues, although that does happen. Most of the time, the negotiation just happens in the course of normal conversation. The negotiation for control offers a good example. Such simple issues as who controls topics of conversation and talking turns emerge immediately. As time goes on, couples negotiate more major control issues, including who makes decisions about finances, children, money, and religion. The next time you observe a couple who has been together for just a short period of time, pay attention to their decision making. Do you notice any signs of negotiation for control?

People negotiate trust when sharing expectations about what constitutes exploitation. Your ability to trust a friend with a secret is based on your expectation that the friend will honor your request for privacy. If your friend violates that expectation and exploits the friendship for his or her own purposes, then trust is up for negotiation. Typically, parties rarely negotiate trust in some abstract sense. They only discuss trust when one party feels used or exploited because he or she expected something different from the other party. At these moments, parties reveal their specific ideas about what constitutes appropriate and inappropriate behavior.

Similarly, couples negotiate intimacy in several ways. On a fairly simple level, you can negotiate intimacy by just smiling and being friendly with someone. Touching someone as a friendly gesture also proposes increased intimacy. Both of these simple gestures ask the person to be friendly back to you. On a more complex level, you can negotiate intimacy through self-disclosing statements. What statement does a person make by disclosing personal information to the other party? They express a desire for increased intimacy. If the other party reciprocates with similar self-disclosures, then both parties succeed in stepping up the intimacy level of the relationship.

In a conflict, parties use these relational features to their advantage. One party might decide to send submissive (give control to the other) and friendly (intimate) messages to increase power. In contrast, the other party might send confrontive (take control of the other) and nasty (nonintimate) messages to increase power. Whatever relational parameters a party selects, that person will often try to impose them on the situation as a means of achieving his or her objectives.

LANGUAGE

Finally, language is a common type of dependency parties try to impose on each other. Language is a formal code for expressing ideas. All people use multiple languages, or codes, when communicating. You may be aware of your body language when communicating. The position of your body, your facial expressions, and even your clothes send a message through a nonverbal code. The emphasis on your words, the dialect you might use, and even the types of words and phrases you select define your verbal codes or languages. How quickly can you switch from one code to another? Can you switch from a code you use with your friends to one more appropriate for formal business situations? Some people switch codes very quickly when they communicate to accomplish several objectives.

During conflict, people typically try to impose their language on the other party. They feel more comfortable with familiar language codes. Have you ever observed police officers in the act of arresting someone? The person under arrest often uses very informal, aggressive, and abusive language. The officers typically use legalistic, formal language to sound more official. This official code carries over into the courtroom and often contrasts sharply with the code defendants use to explain their problem. Negotiators understand that controlling the language means controlling the negotiation. Quite simply, language is the tool parties use to shape issues and structure proposals.

These five levels constitute the social means individuals use to connect with others during a negotiation. Certainly, individuals also connect with each other by sharing various physical objects, as well. A married couple might share a house, children, and a variety of other possessions. Nations might share various kinds of goods and services, manufacturing facilities, or any number of other resources.

The important point is that in any negotiation, the social and physical worlds each represent power bases for individuals. The most successful negotiators use a wide variety of bases for their purposes. Commanding the social as well as the physical environment means understanding power and knowing how to use it. Now, let's take a closer look at how people use power strategically.

❏ Power Strategies

Understanding power strategies means understanding how people manipulate dependencies. For example, if you suffer from low power in a relationship relative to the other person's high power, then you admit your dependency on the other person. You wait for the other person to give you things, structure your thoughts, and possibly direct your life. But if you enjoy high power over your partner, you demonstrate little need for that person's gifts. As a result, dependency on the other person decreases a great deal.

Understanding power strategies means understanding how people manipulate dependencies.

Strategically, as a low-power person, how can you increase your power? Two general options present themselves. First, you can try to increase your partner's dependency on you. You can encourage your partner to express more need for your gifts. Second, you can decrease your dependency on your partner's gifts. These two options outline two general power strategies: *dependency-reducing* and *dependency-expanding* strategies. Let's explore these two strategies; negotiators use them all the time.

DEPENDENCY-EXPANDING SOURCES OF POWER

The goal of dependency-expanding strategies is to increase the other person's dependency on you. You could increase your power by making your partner believe that you have something special to offer. If you succeed and the person wants more of your offerings, then your partner becomes more dependent on you. That increased dependency gives you more power in the relationship.

Credibility

What specific strategies can you use to expand your partner's dependency on you? Perhaps the most common strategy individuals use involves expanding credibility. People view a credible person as competent (knowledgeable and capable), trustworthy (consistently truthful), and dynamic (attractive and interesting). People enhance their credibility by providing needed information in an interesting and attractive fashion. Also, people expand their credibility by exhibiting cultural preferences others like, or embracing ideologies others support. This enhanced credibility creates dependencies by encouraging others to pursue these talents.

Salespeople live by this principle. Every town suffers through car dealers that try their best to exhibit the cultural preferences of their target market. They might try the cowboy approach, if they want to sell pickup trucks in rural areas. They might use upscale, fashionable people, if they want to sell expensive, foreign cars. The strategy is rather transparent: Play up to your viewers whenever possible.

Of course, if listeners see through these ploys, credibility can decrease, costing the speaker power. Violating trust, appearing incompetent, or rejecting the other's culture decreases dependency. Displeasing others compromises credibility. Typically, as interpersonal relationships develop, couples devote a great deal of attention toward enhancing their credibility. They talk about topics of mutual interest, try to respect mutual trust, and build their physical attraction toward the other. As a result, they expand their dependencies on the other and, by definition, wield tremendous power.

Rewards

A second general way of expanding dependencies involves manipulating rewards, or items people value. The most powerful person in a family is often the one that brings in the money. Other powerful people include those who successfully give praise or support to other people. Individuals come to depend on these rewards, making them dependent on the giver. Politicians gain votes by bringing home big projects and lots of jobs to their communities. They encourage the people to depend on them. Of course, this reward dependency can be used against the person by withholding valued rewards. Divorced couples use this strategy frequently by threatening to withhold child visitation if parties fail to meet certain demands. Dependency expands power.

The main advantage of using dependency-expanding sources of power is relationship building. Parties view these strategies as building cooperation. The cooperation balances control while increasing trust and intimacy. Parties communicate their desire not to push but to work with each other when they use these kinds of strategies. The main disadvantage of using dependency-expanding sources of power is time. These strategies are not expedient. Building credibility and establishing a history of giving rewards requires patience. So, when time is a concern, understand that dependency-expanding sources may not prove immediately effective.

DEPENDENCY-REDUCING SOURCES OF POWER

A second general strategy for gaining power in a relationship involves reducing dependencies on others. Rejecting the other's credibility or their rewards, decreases dependency and, in turn, expands relative power. Perhaps you know people who tried to expand their power by saying they wanted out of a relationship. This threat to break up sends the message that the other's rewards are no longer needed. Rejecting the rewards also means rejecting the dependency.

Direct Rejection

Perhaps the most common way of decreasing dependency is direct rejection of the other's offers. Individuals might question the other's credibility or knowledge in a particular area. Lawyers constantly try to persuade the judge and jury that the other party is lying or possesses incomplete information. They ask for direct rejection of the other's information. An even more direct rejection strategy is punishment. Punishing people keeps them in line. It restricts their ability to do things that might add to their power. Divorced individuals frequently punish their ex-spouses by openly flaunting new relationships or turning the children against them.

Indirect Rejection

The second way of reducing the other person's power is to use some other, more covert, means of rejecting the other's offers. A common strategy involves imposing some norm or standard on the other's behavior, again to reduce flexibility and power. Asking the other to play fair or to act like other people encourages the person to stay within some limits. Less flexibility restricts others from trying their own power strategies.

Because this strategy is less direct, it communicates less resistance to the other's power plays. The individual is not seen as the bad guy; the *rules* are the evil culprit forcing change. By not showing so much resistance, the other feels less compelled to retaliate or fight back. Many people hide behind rules as a means of expanding their power. Government bureaucrats owe much of their power to such rules.

The main advantage of using dependency-reducing strategies is expediency. Devaluing the other's offerings instantly gives the speaker more power. However, the main disadvantage of this approach is the cost of this expediency to the relationship. What

Table 5.1 Assessing Power Strategies

Consider the following dialogue from an actual hostage negotiation. Place an R next to those statements that seek to "Reduce" the speaker's dependency on the other person; place an E next to those statements that seek to "Expand" the listener's dependency on the speaker:

_____ 1. Hostage Taker: Get the goddam power in here and bring the goddam sandwiches in here too!

_____ 2. Police Negotiator: Jim, I just found out that the sandwiches have just arrived, and I want to find out from you how you want them delivered.

_____ 3. Hostage Taker: I've already established that. You're really pissing me off. I want them sandwiches brought out now. If someone comes through the window and sticks a gun in, I'll blow up this place. I'm being calm. You all are being a little bit irrational in a type of situation like this. You're not dealing with your average hostage taker.

_____ 4. Police Negotiator: Well, I understand the fact that you're very intelligent, and I appreciate that. We're just about ready to bring the food out to you now. Here's the way it's gonna be done, Jim, now listen up, okay?

_____ 5. Hostage Taker: I told you how it was gonna be done, you tell me how you want to do it and then I'm gonna tell you how it's gonna be done, and I want to know where in the hell my girlfriend is!

---

this strategy really communicates is the speaker's desire to sever ties or decrease interdependence. The move is competitive. It communicates lack of trust and reduced intimacy. If negotiators want to pay that price to achieve their outcomes, then they can use these strategies (Table 5.1).

In the sequence in Table 5.1, you should have placed an E next to the Police Negotiator's statements, and an R next to the Hostage Taker's statements. Typically, in the early phases of hostage negotiation, police rely most consistently on dependency-expanding power strategies. Their goal is to expand their ability to deliver things to the hostage taker. They want the hostage taker to be more dependent on the police. Typically, hostage takers use the more punishing kinds of dependency-reducing strategies, because they do not want to be dependent on the police. Ultimately, they want to escape.

Why should the police avoid dependency-reducing strategies? The police do not want to risk inciting the hostage taker's resistance. After all, they threaten the hostage takers' lives. The police seek to calm hostage takers, while slowly increasing their dependency. Notice in the fourth utterance in Table 5.1 that the Police Negotiator tries tell the Hostage Taker how to do something. The Hostage Taker rejects this dependency-reducing demand very quickly.

USING POWER STRATEGIES

Normally, over the course of an entire bargaining session, negotiators will use both reward-expanding and reward-reducing strategies. Recall from earlier chapters that many conflicts begin with individuals focusing on differences rather than similarities. People are mad at each other and have difficulty working together during the initial periods of conflict. Under these circumstances, negotiators might begin with dependency-reducing strategies in an attempt to devalue what the other has to offer. Socially, the negotiator might try to devalue the other's choice of language codes. "We do not speak that way in these sessions," a negotiator might say in an attempt to alter the other's code. Or the negotiator might devalue the other's ideology or culture to reduce further the other's social bases of power. Even devaluing physical objects the other side controls might be a negotiator's strategy.

If negotiators avoid this initial differentiation phase, they may try to use various dependency-increasing strategies. Many negotiators try to begin sessions by appearing to be a "nice guy." This strategy may include exchanging information to enhance credibility or demonstrating openness to establish trust interpersonally. The negotiator might also try to adopt the other's language code and culture as an expression of goodwill. If parties perceive such moves as genuine, then they might become more dependent.

Of course, as the negotiation progresses, strategies become very intertwined. To extend dependencies, negotiators might try to bolster their own face to portray themselves as knowledgeable and in control of the situation. As each side starts exchanging demands and proposals, the negotiators might begin attacking the other to decrease their credibility and reduce the value of the other side's position. These attacks might become intermixed with more information exchanges and attempts to look strong, competent, and trustworthy. Finally, as an agreement draws near, each side might try to help the other save face so their respective constituents believe they got a good deal. Bolstering the other's credibility is a reward-expanding strategy aimed at improving relations between the sides.

FACTORS INFLUENCING POWER
STRATEGY USE

Three important factors constrain the timing of these power strategies. The first factor is *time*. When negotiators face deadlines, how do they react? When negotiators see high costs for not settling after a certain deadline, they are more likely to move to dependency-reducing strategies. Quite simply, these strategies are more expedient. When time is running out, individuals focus less on the relationship and more on the outcome. They want to control the outcome and forget about building a strong relationship through dependency-increasing strategies.

Second, the *climate* within which parties conduct the negotiations influences the kind of strategies negotiators might use. *Climate* is defined as the degree of cohesiveness among individuals involved in the conflict context. If the parties feel cohesive and the conflict has not raged out of control, then the negotiators are more likely to rely on dependency-increasing strategies. They will try to respect the climate and use strategies that will not generally upset the climate. Many negotiators try to spend some time together before the negotiation actually begins to get to know each other and develop a friendly interpersonal climate. This climate tends to carry over into the negotiations. However, if the parties try to negotiate in a climate of mistrust and hate, then they will turn quickly to dependency-reducing strategies.

The third factor that often influences strategy use is *history*. What kinds of strategies have parties used in the past? Conflicts that have raged for a long time during which parties continuously violate the other's personal needs through dependency-reducing strategies tend to perpetuate themselves with more dependency-reducing strategies. Breaking cycles of uncontrolled conflict escalation is very difficult, as indicated in earlier chapters. Only when a third party helps resolve the problem or when parties face a major external threat do they break this cycle and start using dependency-expanding strategies.

Relative power generally predicts how the conflict will evolve.

Up to this point the focus of this chapter has been on defining power, exploring its dimensions, and expanding on its use. However, for conflict managers, the power problem really comes down to the issue of balance. How much power does each individual possess in the relationship relative to the other? This is an important issue for conflict managers, because relative power generally predicts how the conflict will evolve. Let's discuss the power balance issue because it is central to productive conflict management.

❏ Balancing Power in Relationships

In general, research indicates that individuals best regulate conflict when sharing relatively balanced power. The reason is simple. Balance encourages productivity due to *accountability*. Each side knows that it cannot act with impunity. When not in balance, the stronger party knows that it can act independently to accomplish goals. Balanced power encourages parties to work together to accomplish their goals. Given its importance, let's explore the case supporting power balancing along with effective strategies for achieving it.

THE DANGER IN POWER IMBALANCES

Personal Needs

What happens when power imbalances appear in relationships? Several potentially destructive forces begin to emerge rather quickly. For example, what happens to the personal needs of the weaker party? How much consideration does the more powerful party give to these needs? Remember from the first chapter that when parties fail to grant one another's personal needs, the conflict stays focused on needs and fails to move to substantive issues. The substantive issues get ignored. Clearly, high-power parties pay little attention to the personal needs of the weaker party. Why bother? The high-power party has little need for the low-power party.

So what do low-power parties do in response to this lack of sensitivity and concern for their needs? They might resort to any number of methods to get the attention of high-power parties and ask them to grant their needs. The civil rights movement, which began in the 1950s in the United States, concerned various minority groups asking the white majority to grant basic requests for dignity and respect. Not granting those basic needs encourages low-power parties to escalate the intensity of their requests, which can lead to violence. It is to the credit of Dr. Martin Luther King, Jr., that he sought peaceful, nonviolent means to make such requests and was persistent about them. Clearly, high-power parties need to remain sensitive to the needs of low-power parties to encourage these groups to develop more collaborative approaches to conflict.

Collaboration Difficulty

A second danger associated with power imbalances is that weaker parties are not in a position to pursue a collaborative settlement for two basic reasons. First, collaboration requires that both parties express a willingness to change and become more flexible in their demands. Changing and becoming more flexible means relinquishing some control over outcomes (i.e., relinquishing power). As a result, low-power parties have less to give and thus less flexibility to offer the other party. Think of the problem this way. How much flexibility does a poor person have over how he or she will allocate the monthly budget? Poor people have very little flexibility because the budget must be allocated to the basics every month. Parties enjoy little opportunity to change their behaviors.

Second, collaboration requires that parties focus on the substantive problem at hand. Because the low-power parties in a relationship tend to concentrate on their personal needs, their ability to focus on their interests diminishes considerably. Low-power parties want respect and recognition before they are willing to negotiate the details of some kind of deal.

Problems resulting from power imbalances confront us every day. Many divorces stem from couples who are unable to reconcile power differences. Economic and social oppression feed the violence in our inner cities. Internationally, we see the same problems: Oppressed people rise up in rebellion because they have no other outlet to express their views.

Consider a long-standing conflict between a very powerful nation and its ethnic minority. What does the minority have to lose by engaging in violence? If they have no home and no possessions and their families have been dispersed, what is the cost of violence? They have nothing to lose and something, namely their dignity and cultural identity, to gain. Their lack of power in the relationship precludes them from acting responsibly. If they have something tangible to lose, they will stop the violence. But why do high-power parties feel so reluctant to give power to weaker parties? Perhaps power blinds people to the individual needs of others. Granting needs means giving power to weaker parties and placing them in a position to negotiate in good faith.

PROMOTING POWER BALANCING

Specifically, how can high-power parties give power to those without it? One obvious way is that the high-power parties can make the resources they control more available to all members of society. Resources might include improved economic conditions like lower interest rates, better housing, and productive employment for inner city dwellers.

What about your personal relationships? How can you balance power there? The high-power person can give the other greater control over topics of conversation, critical decisions affecting both parties, and the expression of personal needs. Once high-power parties provide the resources and the training to use those resources, they can begin a more collaborative relationship.

Does this approach work? It works in many settings. Workers in many factories receive increased decision-making responsibilities in their workplace. They have more control over their tasks. Learning to manage this control has increased their commitment to the organization. Courts are now giving divorcing couples more control over their child custody and visitation arrangements through child-custody mediation. The mediation empowers the couples to make their own arrangements. This control encourages them to stick with the plan more closely than if the judge had imposed a plan on them without their input. Indeed, the essence of democracy, and the reason the world is turning to it as its preferred type of government, is that it balances power. Totalitarian governments centralize power in the leadership with no sharing among the people. Such governments fail to endure because they violate basic human needs.

Another way of empowering low-power individuals is to focus on common needs as opposed to individual needs. When individuals focus on the relationship, they become more sensitive and aware of the other's needs. This process is common when an outside source threatens parties in a relationship. That external threat makes people forget about their differences and causes them to focus sharply on what binds them together. For example, labor and management ignore their power differences when threatened by external competition. The American automotive industry has enjoyed such labor-management cooperation and power sharing since foreign competition began to threaten the industry. The kinds of negotiations they experience today focus on common needs and not individual needs. The accountability brought by foreign competition made it happen.

An additional way of empowering low-power parties is generally less complex than the other two. Quite simply, the high-power party can reveal how much power the low-power party really possesses in a relationship. The low-power individual may actually control more than he or she believes. Students typically believe that they remain powerless in their classrooms. However, teachers and administrators know that students have much more power than they typically choose to use. Remember willingness to use power? If 20 or 30 students in a large class rose up to protest a professor's lectures, that professor would experience some difficulty ignoring students' comments in most universities. Many universities empower students to state their views by providing ombudsman services so that students can make formal grievances against faculty and administrators. When a party both controls resources and demonstrates a willingness to use those resources, that party possesses power. Sometimes people need to be reminded that they possess either or both of these power prerequisites.

❑ Conclusions

As indicated at the beginning of this chapter, power plays a very significant role in negotiation. Power relations influence the kinds of opening bids, demands, concessions, and communication strategies that parties select. Indeed, it impacts whether parties are likely to pursue more competitive or collaborative positions in the negotiations. Exactly how power influences negotiations is the subject of the next chapter. However, the important point to learn here is that power is abstract, relational, dynamic, and multidimensional.

Specifically, power relations are abstract in the sense that they generally linger in the background of negotiations until one party tries overtly to manipulate resources. This act removes the abstract "perceptual" quality of power because the manipulator reveals both the resources and the willingness to influence outcomes. Power then becomes a very visible part of the interaction.

Power is also relational in the sense that it derives from one or more relationships among individuals. Understanding power means understanding relationships and how people build or destroy dependencies. Highly interdependent people can greatly influence one another and thus wield tremendous power over one another. Virtual strangers have very little power over each other because they cannot influence the other's life. Picking a fight with a stranger demonstrates dependency on that stranger. Clearly, the person could not achieve satisfaction without picking the fight. Explore your own dependencies carefully and you will find very interesting power relationships.

Because dependencies are dynamic, power is dynamic. Change can come quickly or slowly to power relationships. This is certainly true on the international front. Very unusual bonds can form quickly among nations when they have a common enemy to fight. Countries that were once enemies, or perhaps strangers, can become friends and hold tremendous power over one another. Countries can also change their dependencies on physical resources such as raw materials and technology.

Finally, power is multidimensional because dependencies are multidimensional. People negotiate power and dependencies through cultures, ideologies, institutions, relationships, and languages. These negotiations are often very difficult to understand, but are very profound. Persuading another person to accept your culture and ideology, for example, makes that other person more dependent on you, forcing him or her to play your game. Effective negotiators remain sensitive to the idea that dependencies emerge from several directions. In the next chapter, we will see how negotiators translate this knowledge into action.

Negotiating in the Face of Power

Chapter 5 made the point that the first step in understanding negotiation is understanding power. This relationship is tight because power is always an issue when people communicate. Each comment negotiators make either reinforces dependencies in place or tries to alter those dependencies. Recall the dependency-expanding and -reducing strategies discussed in Chapter 5? Even if one party simply gives the other some information, that act seeks to expand the other's dependence on the person giving the information. These power strategies hide in the subtle nature of negotiation. Of course, when parties make demands or use coercion, power strategies become more apparent and easier to recognize. The important point to remember is that power serves as the foundation for building negotiation strategies and tactics.

The significance of power becomes quickly apparent in hostage negotiation. In hostage negotiations, even the most innocent comment can make a big power play. In a recent airplane hijacking, the hijacker asked the police negotiators for hamburgers to feed himself and the passengers. The police asked what he wanted on the burgers. Can you imagine asking this kind of question at that moment? Who cares what he wants on the burgers? However, the request was very intentional on the part of the police. They wanted the hijacker to believe that the police genuinely wanted to meet his demands. This dependency-expanding strategy begins building a relationship that the police can use to make more demands later in the negotiations. So the police gave the hostage taker the opportunity to demand and receive more stuff, like pickles and catsup. Thus an apparently innocent comment can play a very important role in altering power relationships in a negotiation.

Clearly, negotiators pay close attention to power issues during all phases of negotiation. They can't afford not to. Because of this important connection, this chapter seeks to integrate the concepts of power and negotiation strategy. Before we can explore that integration fully, we need to begin with a basic understanding of the negotiation context. Specifically, what factors influence the context and how can we take control of them?

❏ Personal Factors Affecting the Negotiation Context

The first question any negotiator must ask is whether the parties are ready to cut a deal. Are they ready to bargain in good faith? If parties can control their emotions and focus on the task, they are ready to begin. So what kind of negotiation context do you wish to create: *competitive* or *collaborative*? You discovered in Chapter 3 that to some extent this is an irrelevant question because most conflicts begin competitively. The parties focus on their own interests while blaming the other for the problems dividing them. These external attributions of blaming the other forces parties to defend against these personal attacks. If parties fail to retain their task focus, this competitive context can quickly degenerate into a needs-centered fight. Recall the hostage negotiation interaction from the last chapter and the competitive comments forwarded by the hostage taker listed in Table 5.1. What if the police had responded to the hostage taker's comments with defensive statements? The police might have jeopardized the hostages' lives. Only when negotiators finally realize that looking toward the future is in both parties' best interests can they start to work more collaboratively.

The best way to succeed in negotiation is to decide what kind of context you want right from the beginning.

So to some extent, negotiators cannot control the extent to which a negotiation turns more collaborative or competitive. Quite naturally, people tend to move back and forth between these two approaches. However, the best way to succeed in negotiation is to decide what kind of context you want right from the beginning. This decision starts your game plan. It outlines your path to success. Only when the path is clear can you take control of the interaction and move it in the best direction.

Is one context always best? Clearly, one will not work in all situations. Your best context depends on several factors. Use the set of factors discussed below as a checklist when planning your negotiations.

YOUR GOALS

Examine your goals. Clear goals promote cooperativeness because they:

1. Provide a specific focus and direction for the discussion.
2. Specify when parties have resolved an issue or made a decision.
3. Help individuals coordinate their needs.

In contrast, unclear goals promote more destructive communication. What happens when people enter conflict with no clear idea of what they want? Are they more likely to focus on their future needs or dwell on the past? They will most likely dwell on the past. Goals keep the focus on the future and what parties need to resolve the conflict. Not forming goals often turns a negotiation session into a yelling match. When there are no goals, people are encouraged to dwell on how the *other party* caused all the problems. You know the effect of these personal attributions. They threaten personal needs and derail constructive problem solving. Clear goals *not aimed at hurting the other party* keep the focus on the future and provide more incentive to cooperate.

Another disadvantage of unclear goals is exploitation. By not knowing what you want, you are implicitly asking the other side to tell you what you want. Will they define your goal in your best interests? Perhaps they will. But if they do not, then parties risk compromising trust and stimulating competition.

The primary positive effect of clear goals is balanced power. Neither side has the advantage of determining goals. Each side shares that responsibility and begins from that position. Balanced power helps promote cooperativeness, because both sides must work together to get what they want from the interaction.

YOUR RELATIONSHIP

If you care about preserving the relationship between yourself and the other party, then confronting the conflict is important. Confrontation means you want to clear the air so the relationship can progress. In negotiation, the same principle is true. If you value the relationship, pursuing a collaborative negotiation context is important. As you know from the discussion of conflict styles, collaborative relationships show concern for the other party. Showing concern for the other's needs builds relationships in the long run. Clearly, valuing the relationship means pursuing collaboration.

YOUR SKILLS

How comfortable are you with your communication and negotiation skills? Confronting a conflict productively depends in large measure on your communication skills. When faced with a problem, do you quickly run out of words and want to leave or escape the situation? If so, you might lack the communication and negotiation skills needed to respond collaboratively to situations. Communication skills needed for a collaborative approach to negotiation include reframing, active listening, and structuring your conversation. More negotiation-related skills are discussed later in this chapter.

YOUR TIME

Finally, if negotiators face time deadlines, they are more likely to react competitively. Potential losses loom more significantly as time goes on. Many negotiators try to prolong the negotiation process so people can take plenty of time to explore options and develop collaborative approaches to problem solving. Hostage negotiators believe that time works in favor of the police, because it gives hostage takers time to calm down and think more rationally. The last thing hostage negotiators want is speed. They never rush the hostage taker.

❑ Strategic Factors Affecting the Negotiation Context

Assume that you wish to build a collaborative negotiation situation. You set about meeting the requirements for building this situation: You construct clear goals, you place a high value on the relationship, you assess your communication skills, and you make sure the negotiators have plenty of time to interact. But what if the other person does not reciprocate these factors? What if he or she seeks a competitive context? What you must realize is that you can have a powerful impact on a negotiation by taking the lead and steering the negotiation in a cooperative direction. You must decide what kind of context you wish to create. Even if your partner initially wants a different kind of negotiation session, you can steer it in the direction you want.

The reason is the principle of reciprocation. In communication, people tend to mirror one another's style of communicating. Acts of competition stimulate other acts of competition. Use this principle in your favor. Decide what kind of communication approach you want, then try to move it in that direction. Professional negotiators—including lawyers, labor leaders, and sports agents—

know this principle. They decide well in advance of the session what kind of context they want to create, then they set about creating it. Consider the following elements in building your negotiation strategy.

OPPORTUNITY TO COMMUNICATE

Communication channels exert an important impact on negotiation (Putnam & Poole, 1987). A communication channel is the medium through which people exchange information. The most common channel we use is face-to-face communication. This channel carries a great deal of information, because we can see, hear, and touch the person if we choose. Written documents restrict the communication channel because parties can only see words. Written messages miss the nonverbal emphasis on certain words, the intensity of the message, and eye contact.

What effect does channel restriction exert on competitiveness? Research reveals that increasing restrictions also increases competitiveness. You probably experienced this effect if you ever participated in a long-distance relationship. You probably found that the phone was not a very satisfying way of carrying on a relationship. It is hard to show someone how you feel when using restricted communication channels. Face-to-face communication works to inform the

Providing opportunities to interact before bargaining begins also serves to build a collaborative context.

individuals about the relationship. It gives people an opportunity to tell if they can trust each other, because the primary information people use to determine trust is visual. We use eye contact and body posture as signs of truth telling. When information about trust is not available, most people think the worst. They feel more vulnerable to exploitation. Restricted communication, like letters and phone calls, makes it more difficult to send the subtle messages that instill a sense of trust in the other party.

Providing opportunities to interact before bargaining begins also serves to build a collaborative context. Informal communication before formal negotiations helps parties get to know each other on a personal basis. This personal contact in an unstressful situation allows parties to build up trust. In addition, it gives parties a chance to learn about the other's goals and generally creates an open atmosphere. The best way to build a collaborative context involves trying informal communication before the formal session begins.

INFORMATION EXCHANGE

Research also reveals many interesting results about the influence of information exchange on building a collaborative context. Bargainers who know their opponent's limitations are more altruistic, or more willing to be nice to the opponent. You might expect that revealing your limitations would make you more vulnerable to attack. Oddly enough, it has the opposite effect. When others know your limitations, they want to respond collaboratively. Again, the explanation goes back to the principle of reciprocation. Openness tends to breed more openness.

However, take caution not to overload the other party with too much information about yourself and your position in a negotiation. Too much information makes it difficult for the other party to understand your position. They might see too much information as a smoke screen and assume you are doing it to hide your true intentions. This ambiguity can create competition by building suspicion about your intentions. The recommendation for building a collaborative context is to give relevant and honest information about your situation. This move puts tremendous pressure on the other person to do the same and, ultimately, results in collaboration.

MESSAGE STRATEGIES AND TACTICS

Message strategies and tactics also send messages about competition. In general, negotiators can pick from two strategies: hardline and softline. A *hardline* approach has the following characteristics:

1. An initial offer that significantly exceeds the individual's goals; however, this offer should not offend the other or motivate him or her to withdraw from the negotiations.

2. Infrequent concessions that are given only in response to the opponent's concessions; giving concessions without waiting for the opponent to concede generally communicates weakness and the other party assumes that the negotiator wants to settle quickly or has a weak case.

3. Frequent persuasive arguments aimed at convincing the other that the initial offer is valid and should be accepted; these arguments might focus on the weaknesses of the other's position or the strength of the negotiator's position and might also point out situational problems that require a prompt settlement.

Look at the implications of this approach. What hidden messages do bargainers send when they take the hardline path? The very first message sent when parties make offers is, "I am not going to tell you what I really want. You have to guess what I really want." This lack of openness reinforces a context that lacks trust and openness. It assumes that individuals want to maximize their own gains and minimize the other's. The infrequent-concession strategy plays the same game by seeing who can hold out longer. Again, the goal is to win regardless of the other's needs. So by selecting this general approach, the bargainer creates a competitive negotiation context that treats the outcome as more important than the relationship. It sacrifices the relationship in favor of the outcome.

In contrast, a *softline* approach has the following characteristics:

1. An initial offer that is less than desired, but encourages the other to reciprocate with some token offer; an initial offer that is easy for both sides to accept tries to get the negotiation rolling in a collaborative direction.

2. Conceding first or accepting the other's token offer to show cooperation and to encourage the other to accept the first token offer.

3. A thorough explanation about the motivations underlying the first concession; specifically, the negotiator explains that the concession represents a desire for more trust and collaboration. Not providing the explanation might be interpreted as a sign of weakness and might encourage the other to pursue a hardline bargaining approach.

Softline approaches reshape the bargaining context by talking first about issues rather than proposals.

The hardline approach is called *proposal-based bargaining*, because it begins with each side making specific proposals for ending the negotiations. This approach establishes a competitive context not only for the reasons cited above but because bargainers must also deal with the inherent face-threatening nature of proposal-based bargaining. From another perspective, once you start with your best offer, any subsequent offers must, by definition, ask for something less than what you want. This concession means a loss of face as bargainers appear weaker for giving in to the opponent.

The softline strategy is called *issue-based bargaining*, because it typically begins not with proposals, but with a discussion of key issues separating parties. In this preliminary discussion, the parties do not attach any numbers of specific ways of resolving the negotiations. They simply express concerns they might have and keep the discussion on that level. Later on, after reaching some consensus about the issues, they begin the proposal process with the softline strategy.

As you might suspect, this process works to build more collaboration, because it opens up communication. It sends the message that the long-term health of the parties' relationship is of primary importance. By selecting the softline approach, the bargainer, in effect, requests increased collaboration. Given these two broad types of negotiation contexts, what kind of communication context do you wish to create? Do you want a collaborative or competitive context (Table 6.1)? Now consider your preferences in light of a set of rules for conducting both collaborative and competitive negotiation.

COMPETITIVE NEGOTIATION STRATEGIES

Opening Bid

A competitive, or distributive, negotiation context operates with a fairly rigid set of informal rules about demands, concessions, opening bids, and argument structure. The reason for this

Table 6.1 Assessing Your Negotiation Preferences

This questionnaire will help you assess whether you generally prefer to pursue more competitive or more collaborative negotiation contexts. Indicate the degree to which you engage in the following behaviors.

If you "Never" engage in the behavior, answer 1;

if you "Seldom" engage in the behavior, answer 2;

if you "Sometimes" engage in the behavior, answer 3;

if you "Often" engage in the behavior, answer 4;

if you "Always" engage in the behavior, answer 5.

When I negotiate, I

_____ try to win.

_____ try to win, but if I can't, I make sure the other person can't win either.

_____ blame the other person for the problem.

_____ discredit the other person's position.

_____ conceal my true intentions.

Add the numbers next to each statement. Scores range from 5 to 25. The higher the score, the more you prefer competitive negotiation. Now, complete the next set of statements, which ask about your collaborative negotiation desires. Respond to these statements using the same answering system as above.

When I negotiate, I

_____ work toward a solution both parties like.

_____ reveal my true intentions at the beginning of the negotiation.

_____ give the first concession.

_____ remain flexible on the means of reaching a solution.

_____ refrain from personally attacking the other negotiator.

Again, add the numbers next to each statement. Scores range from 5 to 25. The higher the score, the more you prefer collaborative negotiation.

rigidity is that this context is the most commonly observed form of negotiation, at least among Western cultures. I hope that you are able to play the game well.

Rule 1 for distributive negotiation is *Your opening bid should be just under the point of insulting the opponent.*

If you make demands that are insulting or threatening, the opponent might withdraw. Or if you make a bid that is too low, the opponent might accept quickly, indicating that you could have received more. The issue really revolves around structuring the opening bid. Structuring this bid must be based on:

1. Your expectations of the other's opening bid or his or her ultimate demand. Part of the art of distributive negotiation involves estimating what the other person will ask for and what he or she really wants from the negotiations. The more information gained about the other's likely opening bid and bottom line (the lowest level of settlement) the easier it is to structure an opening bid.

2. Your perceptions of the strength of your own position. The stronger you perceive your own case, the more likely you will escalate your opening bid. If you think your case is weak for any reason (e.g., you hold a weaker image or you offer fewer desirable items), you might ask for something that the opponent can accept immediately. Of course, the opponent also understands this condition and will be looking very carefully at your opening bid to see if you believe your case is strong.

3. Your available time. Again, if you begin with a high opening bid and impose a time deadline on the opponent, you send a very clear message to your opponent that says, "I have a strong case." If you want to pump up the perceived strength of your case, a high opening bid accompanied by a take-it-or-leave-it attitude accomplishes that goal. Nevertheless, time definitely shapes perceptions of an opening bid.

Rule 2 for negotiation deals with timing: *Try to avoid giving the first opening bid.*

Let your opponent give the bid. The reasons should be obvious. The opening bid reveals a great deal of information. It communicates what the negotiators think about their own position relative to their opponent's position. For example, a strong opening bid with time deadlines says, "I think my position is stronger than yours, otherwise I would not risk such a strong offer." Because position strength information plays such an important role in negotiation, try to wiggle out of giving an opening bid. Let your opponent go first, then come back with your own opening bid. The downside of this strategy is that it communicates an inability to trust the opponent to be open with you. Clearly, negotiators must handle this process with some political skill by giving the other person many reasons why they should go first. Certainly, if you know a great deal about the other's likely opening bid, then you can go first and try to develop some trust between the parties.

The following dialogue from an actual labor-management negotiation illustrates the tricky problem of giving the opening bid. Again, the negotiation dance involves trying to refuse to do something cooperatively. See how they execute this dance

LABOR: [after an *opening statement by management*] Thanks for that interesting opening statement. I guess what we're interested in knowing right now is, are you prepared to give us some numbers on the salary issue so we have a firm grip on where we stand on that issue?

MANAGEMENT: I think that's fair. I think what we would be most interested in is your views on those numbers.

LABOR: Okay, we're not going to get hung up on the whole question of exchanging specific numbers. We are just interested in ballpark figures at this point.

MANAGEMENT: Let's put it this way. Let's hear what you have to say, and then at that point we will commit if we're going to indicate exactly where we're at. Why don't you just share with us what you've got?

Wasn't that an intricate and entertaining dance? Each party tries to sidestep the other in a nice way. Giving the opening bid reveals so much about a team's position that neither labor nor management wanted to show its cards first. Even though the dance is nice, it still signals a competitive context and sets the stage for later negotiations.

Rule 3 involves concession timing: *Under most circumstances, avoid conceding first.*

Concessions

In a competitive negotiation, the opponent will read the concession as an indication that you believe your position is weak. After all, what else could have motivated the concession? The preferred strategy is to concede only in response to the opponent's concession and only as often as the opponent concedes. This reciprocated concession sends the message that you are willing to work with the person and not stonewall him or her. If you do not reciprocate after a reasonable period of time, then the other party will think you are uncooperative, and you risk being too firm. Some fairness must enter the negotiations.

Even though Rule 3 encourages you to concede only in response to your opponent, first concessions work under some conditions. To ease tension, you might provide the opponent with a small concession on a relatively insignificant point. You probably used this strategy as a child. Many children ask for several kinds of treats and hold out for the one treat they really want. Conceding the other treats puts pressure on the parents to provide the most desired treat. Professional negotiators understand this principle very well. They combine trivial demands with important demands so they have something easy to give up.

Also, if you seem to be running out of time and you need to get the ball rolling, a first concession is a way to accomplish that goal. However, if this first concession is major, it reveals your second most preferred position and gives the opponent a great deal of information about you.

Rule 4 deals with concession rates: *Try to keep your concessions fairly minimal.*

Large concessions indicate that you believe your position is weak for some reason. You can avoid sending that message by giving only fairly small concessions, particularly if the negotiations are moving along at a satisfactory pace. Again, if the atmosphere grows tense, then a small concession might be needed to create the impression that the negotiator wants to make progress and bargain in good faith. In general, communicating progress is important because it motivates the opponent to keep bargaining with you.

The size of the first concession also reveals a fair amount of information about your *best alternative to a negotiated agreement* (BATNA). If your opponent's first concession is fairly small, then it seems that the person has other alternatives to negotiation. Of course, the small concession might be a bluff to encourage you to give a concession so your opponent can assess your BATNA. Regardless of the true intention of the first concession, remain aware of the amount of information contained in the first concession. It's very important.

Arguments

Several rules need to be defined with respect to argument qualities. Arguments are the reasons or justifications for your positions. Bargainers spend most of their time in negotiation exchanging arguments, thus you should understand some basic, commonly accepted rules.

Rule 5 is *Support your own position first, then worry about the other's position.*

Above all, make your position strong and clear. If you don't, you increase your vulnerability and invite your opponent to think you are unprepared. So it is important to be exhaustive in your knowledge of the facts with plenty of background information. The facts must be well organized and to the point. Most often, the most well prepared negotiator comes out ahead.

Rule 6 is *Make sure that the information you use to support your position is capable of persuading your opponent.*

Avoid justifications or facts that the person finds uninteresting or irrelevant. Try to learn as much about the person's attitudes, values and beliefs and tailor your arguments to his or her views. Visualize a negotiation in which the parties almost deadlock. Suddenly, a negotiator starts talking about his military experience. The other party looks surprised and indicates that he greatly respects military people. From that point on, the veteran enjoys increased credibility. This credibility automatically makes his arguments more persuasive. Learning your opponent's values can significantly increase your credibility and enhance your leverage in a negotiation.

Rule 7 is *Don't threaten or attack your opponent and, if you must, make sure you do it only as a last resort.*

How do threats to use your power impact your power? Recall from Chapter 5 that threats work in the short term if your opponent believes that you can and will carry out the threat.

However, you also send some potentially dangerous messages when you use threats. First, you send the message that you must use force because you could not get your way through less-confrontive means. In a sense, you are less powerful than before you made the threat for two reasons. You communicate that you are ineffective strategically; you cannot control your opponent any other way. Also, you communicate that your BATNA is not very good when you make threats. The threat indicates that you are desperate and do not have a good alternative to negotiation. As a result, you lose both credibility and flexibility. By communicating this information, your opponent might become even more unwilling to change, particularly if the opponent's BATNA is better than yours. Just be aware that using threats or force can take away some of your power.

Second, you send the message that you are no longer interested in cooperating with the other party. You want compliance now, not later. You do not care about the relationship. This severe escalation in conflict may encourage the opponent to withdraw from the situation, particularly if the opponent's BATNA is high. The point here is to use threats cautiously because they might do more harm than good.

COLLABORATIVE NEGOTIATION STRATEGIES

Setting the Stage

Because the collaborative negotiation process is much less rigid than the distributive context, the number of rules governing the process is much smaller; therefore, only a few basic rules will be provided here. Collaborative, or softline, strategies involve exchanging information about goals and issues rather than specific proposals. How do bargainers set the stage for this information exchange? They might first begin by detailing the issues they want to discuss in the negotiations.

Rule 1 is *Be prepared to identify clearly the specific issues you want to resolve during the negotiations.*

Remember, in collaborative negotiation, each party commits to helping the other obtain his or her goals. To achieve this objective, the parties must first commit to learning what divides them. What are the specific barriers to an agreement? Disclosing all the issues dividing parties sets the stage for opening up information exchange and laying the groundwork for making proposals.

Stating Proposals

As you may recall, collaborative negotiation does not mean compromising goals. To the contrary, it means standing firm. Why choose a negotiation strategy that necessarily compromises goals? Collaboration simply means that negotiators help each other accomplish the goals. As a result, the key to working together is remaining flexible about the means you use to accomplish your goals.

Rule 2 is *Remain firm about your goals, but flexible about your methods.*

Offer to help the other party accomplish his or her goals while indicating flexibility in methods. For example, Pruitt (1981) defines several methods for constructing proposals that aim toward collaboration. To illustrate the point, consider two hungry children negotiating over who will eat an apple they recently acquired. In a strategy called *log rolling,* the children take turns helping each other satisfy their hunger. Using this strategy, the children would decide who is most hungry, and that child would get the first apple. The child who gets the apple then agrees to help the other find a second apple as soon as possible. So log rolling is really a turn-taking strategy; parties agree to help each other alternatively.

A second collaborative strategy is called *cost-cutting.* In this strategy, each party agrees to help the other avoid the costs associated with helping each other accomplish the goals. For example, what if some other children are watching the children negotiate for the apple? The child who agrees to give the apple might express fear that the children watching the negotiation might ridicule the child giving up the apple. In this circumstance, the child who eats the first apple agrees to tell the observing children something that will help the child giving up the apple to feel better. Following this episode, the children might also agree to log roll their problem and go find another apple or something equally desirable.

A third strategy consists of *broadening the pie.* This strategy means working creatively to expand the potential outcomes. Using this strategy, our hungry children might try to sell the apple or exchange it for something that would satisfy both their hungers. This strategy is generally the most difficult because it requires the most creativity, trust, and patience of any collaborative strategy. However, it can be the most effective, because it looks to expand potential outcomes so parties can exceed their goals.

You probably noticed that these collaborative strategies require:

1. Extensive communication skills. Parties must be able to listen to each other and stick to the issues while avoiding needs-centered personal attacks.
2. Face-to-face communication to build trust and stimulate creative problem solving.
3. Honest goal sharing so parties can really help each other. That is, parties must be willing to say what they really want. For example, did the child really want the apple to satisfy hunger? Or did the child need to save face and maintain power? Fundamental, under-

lying goals are difficult to identify, but it's mandatory for collaborative negotiation to work.

Rule 3 for collaborative negotiation involves focus: *Attack only the issues and not the other person.*

Arguments

Be forceful about your feelings related to the issues. Intense language communicates a strong commitment to your objectives. Avoid personal attacks because the whole purpose behind collaborative negotiation is building relationships. You want to strengthen your relationship through bargaining by showing the other person you care about his or her needs. Attacking the other's personal needs violates this advantage. As a result, arguments should focus on the issues raised during the initial phases of negotiation.

❑ Negotiation and Power

How does power affect the way in which negotiators manipulate these competitive and collaborative bargaining strategies? Recall that power refers to the relative control of resources. The more powerful person in a relationship controls more resources. By this definition, the more powerful person enjoys more flexibility in a negotiation. He or she can more easily influence both the outcomes and the methods used to achieve those outcomes. However, this potential influence works very differently in competitive and collaborative negotiations. To understand the difference, it is important to examine each approach carefully.

POWER IN COMPETITIVE NEGOTIATIONS

Negotiators in competitive negotiations lust after power because they want the ability to dictate outcomes to the opponent. In other words, they wish to maintain, and even widen, the power imbalance in negotiations. A high-power party will enjoy a favorable BATNA and not really need to negotiate if the other party starts showing too much resistance. As a result, the high-power person's concessions will be much smaller and less frequent. In fact, people often reveal power by not conceding a bit from their very high offer.

High-power people also want to control the process of interaction. Specifically, they wish to impose their culture and ideology on the other party. In addition, they would like to dictate the institutional and relational parameters parties will use during negotiations. Similarly, they will try to impose their own language on the negotiations, because they are most comfortable with this language. The high-power person wants to play on his or her home turf with his or her own ball. This person seeks to stack the deck to enhance flexibility in dictating settlement terms. In fact, the high-power person's goal generally extends to avoiding negotiation altogether. If that person gains sufficient power, negotiation is not necessary—the person simply takes what he or she wants.

POWER IN COLLABORATIVE NEGOTIATIONS

Negotiators in collaborative negotiations seek a different set of power relations. They wish to balance power among parties. The high-power person tries to empower the other party to participate in the negotiations. Why should the high-power person give up power? The answer lies in taking a long-term perspective regarding negotiation. In a collaborative negotiation, the high-power person realizes that power can be a very temporary phenomenon. It can go away tomorrow, particularly if the other party in the relationship gets too upset with the high-power person and terminates the relationship. As a result, negotiators should take a long-term perspective of the negotiation process. They should work toward building an equal partnership that helps both parties create something they could not build individually.

Remember the children with the apple? Assume that the apple belonged to one of the children. If the owner gave the apple to the other child in return for a promise to help in finding more food, the owner accomplishes two goals. The owner increases the chances of getting more food and strengthens a friendship. Relationship building, the main priority for the collaborative negotiator, develops only in a balanced power relationship. In the competitive relationship, the negotiator expresses little care about the relationship; the goal is the priority.

Parties also negotiate the process of communication during a collaborative interaction. Each party tries to find a culture; an ideology; and a set of institutional, relational, and linguistic parameters they both find useful. Actually, the high-power person might even allow the other to dictate some of these parameters to level power once again. The aim is never to force the other party to accept anything. The purpose involves paying lots of attention to power imbalances and correcting them so the relationship can develop. Recall how setting the stage is so important in collaborative interaction. Setting the stage is another term for building a solid relationship before bargaining.

❏ Conclusions

Clearly, power and negotiation live together very intimately. As a result, an expert negotiator is also an expert in power. To illustrate this intimate relationship, consider the challenge divorce mediators face when trying to help a divorcing couple negotiate child custody and visitation issues. Mediators generally try to build a collaborative relationship between parties during the mediation process. They hope the parents will work together cooperatively to raise the child. Mediators look for power imbalances. In terms of the couple's history, they examine who initiated the divorce, and how much each party wants to break up the marriage. They monitor who controls the conversation, who makes all the proposals, and who is the most skilled communicatively. If they sense any large discrepancies in these attributes, they quickly try to help the low-power party work through his or her deficiencies so he or she can contribute equally to the negotiations. Power is always on the mediator's mind because it is so central to the quality of the negotiations.

For the novice negotiator, the challenges are great. Detecting power differences and determining their nature is difficult enough. Then, the person must decide what kind of negotiation strategy to pursue. If a collaborative approach seems desirable, then the person must determine how to empower the other party. These are difficult tasks and probably are mastered only through much practice. The purpose of this chapter is to outline some options for you in this regard. The competitive strategy is not always good, or necessary, and neither is the collaborative approach. Each has its place. The skilled negotiator knows when and how to use each approach. Just understanding the differences is an important first step. Perfecting them is the real challenge.

7

What Kind of
Conflict Help Is Available?

By now, you probably see yourself as a negotiation expert. Actually, negotiation, like all communication contexts, requires extensive experience to realize success. Nevertheless, the basic overview in Chapter 6 should enable you to take control of your negotiation activities.

What if your negotiation efforts fail? What if the negotiation regresses to a needs-centered discussion and escalates into verbal, or even physical, aggression? Many people use a third party to help intervene in disputes that escalate out of control. Third parties work best when both disputants agree to use them in a valid attempt at problem solving.

Unfortunately, many people reject third-party help. One person in a marriage may want to see a counselor, but the other party refuses. Or a judge might force people to use a third party only to see them sabotage the third party's efforts.

This chapter assumes that both parties want to seek a third party's help. But which third-party role works best for which kinds of disputes? This chapter provides this information. It focuses on the kinds of help available to people when their negotiation fails. To begin this discussion, it is necessary to define the third-party role.

❏ Defining the Third-Party Role

A third party is a neutral individual who enters a conflict with the goal of assisting parties to manage their conflict. This definition is very important because it outlines some basic features of the third-party role. The first feature to consider is *neutrality*. A third party should approach the conflict as a neutral with no vested interest in the outcome. The third party wishes to side with no one. And the outcome should not personally affect that third party.

A judge in a court of law is a third party. And the judge does not personally benefit from his or her decision about a case. The judge applies objective criteria in making a decision about the conflict. In contrast, consider a family conflict, perhaps between a mother and a daughter. If the father steps in the middle, is the father truly neutral? Can the father claim objectivity? In all likelihood, the father's relationship with both parties compromises neutrality. Both the mother and child might blame the father for the outcome; this blame could personally affect the father's life. So he finds it difficult to remain neutral and objective. A true third party sustains an objective position at all costs to avoid these kinds of problems.

The second feature of the definition addresses the issue of how the third party *enters* the conflict. In most cases, the disputants ask the third party for help because they cannot process the conflict by themselves. However, in other cases, the third party must enter the conflict. For example, the law requires that only judges can dissolve a marriage. Ministers cannot dissolve marriages. Legal restrictions force the judge to address the conflict.

The third important feature of the definition deals with the third party's goal. In general, a third party seeks to *assist* parties to manage their conflict. What does *assist* really mean? Assisting might mean passively directing couples to think about some issues dividing them. Or assisting could include the very directive action of legally dissolving a marriage. Third parties must identify an appropriate intervention role and decide what specific intervention to use in that situation. Most third parties assume one kind of role and rarely jump from one role to another. For example, ministers and counselors remain in their specific roles, because other roles require very different kinds of skills. If the parties' resolution needs change, they generally move to a different person, who is trained to address these new needs.

Fourth, third parties help parties to *manage* their conflict, not solve their conflict. The difference between managing and solving the conflict is important. For instance, some courts encourage parents and their runaway children to mediate their differences. The parent and child often enter mediation in full agreement. The parent rejects the child and the child rejects the parent. Here, mediators try to create conflict about goals so parties can talk about the problem. They want to stimulate conflict to stimulate problem solving. In such a case, the issue focuses on helping parties manage an ongoing conflict about their needs. Resolving the conflict fails to meet the parties' needs.

What kind of third-party roles can negotiators request when they need some help? The following section identifies four primary roles: conciliator, mediator, arbitrator, and adjudicator. The various features of these different roles are detailed in Table 7.1.

❏ Types of Third-Party Roles

CONCILIATOR

Goals

As you can see from Table 7.1, conciliators help parties sort out their relational problems. As you know from earlier chapters,

Table 7.1 Third-Party Roles

Type	Goals	Structure	Contexts
Conciliator	1. Relational stability 2. Disputant controlled	1. Informal 2. Quite variable	1. Psychologists 2. Social workers 3. Religious 4. Friends/relatives 5. Counselors/therapists
Mediator	1. Resolve specific problem 2. Disputant controlled	1. Somewhat formal, but highly flexible 2. Generally specific process used	1. Divorce/family 2. Criminal/civil 3. Community 4. Environmental 5. Educational 6. Labor
Arbitrator	1. Decide problem for parties 2. Not binding 3. Third party controls outcomes	1. Fairly formal process—each side talks, the arbitrator decides 2. Arbitrators have fair latitude about rules	1. Family/divorce 2. Labor 3. Consumer/community
Adjudicator	1. Make a legally binding outcome 2. To solve a legal problem	1. Very formal—specific rules and laws covering all of the processes	1. Court structures vary from area to area 2. Many types (district, circuit, probate, appeals, federal, and supreme)

relational problems create the most frustrating challenges for people because of their abstract qualities. What is a trust or intimacy problem, how did it start, and how can it be managed? Conciliators help parties sort through these difficult questions. They seek to decrease relational ambiguity and help parties decide what kind of relationship they want in the future.

Strategies	Advantages	Disadvantages	Recommendations
1. Feelings based, not problem based	1. Needed for productive interaction	1. Takes time 2. Emotionally difficult 2. Good to take stock—adjust to change	1. Use proactively 2. If not, go in as soon as possible 3. Often done too late
1. Focus on problem— relationship secondary	1. Parties control outcomes 2. Fairly successful 3. Less costly than other models	1. Success difficult with relationship problems 2. Success differs with power discrepancies	1. Use for a specific problem 2. Check qualifications 3. Use before court option to preserve relationship
1. Gather information/ decide outcome 2. No focus on relationship issues	1. Speed/ efficiency 2. Effective when outcome is needed and relationship is not a problem	1. Probably overused 2. Third-party controlled	1. Use after more cooperative alternative to solve problem 2. Use before court 3. Use when a quick outcome is desired
1. Gather evidence 2. Determine facts 3. Make a decision	1. Need a final option that ends the process	1. Third-party controlled 2. Not good in values conflict	1. Use as a last resort 2. Use attorneys/ shop around 3. Be an active participant in the process; be a good client

For example, many judges ask divorcing parties to seek conciliation before divorce so they can negotiate their separation. Many couples who use divorce mediation first try conciliation. They must achieve at least some kind of working relationship so they can speak directly to each other in the same room.

In conciliation, the disputants totally control the outcome. The competent conciliator never tells parties what kind of relationship they ought to have. Conciliators simply ask questions and provide information to create insights for the parties. They also suggest strategies for addressing relational needs.

Structure

Conciliators assume the least-formal type of third-party role. They use few standard rules and procedures. The conciliator simply goes with the flow and tries to uncover important insights that might help the parties. The approaches that conciliators use are quite variable. Some conciliators take a fairly structured approach that moves parties through specific phases of interaction. Others use no set pattern of intervention. The differences reflect different philosophies and perspectives on how to help people come to grips with their relational problems.

Contexts

Conciliators come in many forms. Many are psychologists or social workers trained to deal with family or marital relationships. Some are religious leaders who deal with the relational problems of their members. These counselors and therapists provide valuable assistance in helping people identify their relational needs. Perhaps the most common type of conciliator is a friend or relative. Family members often place their own relatives in the middle of disputes, which can add to the problem. After all, family and friends offer the most convenient source of support in difficult times. How often do you seek advice from a friend or family member? Have you ever asked one to intervene in a conflict?

Strategies

Counselors and therapists use many creative strategies to access feelings and relational orientations. They might begin with straightforward questions and then move to more intensive strategies designed to reveal deep feelings. Some conciliators use role-playing for this purpose so each party can see how he or she views

the other's role. Or a counselor might try confrontation to encourage parties to express their true
feelings. Regardless of the approach, *The primary advan-*
conciliators focus only on relational *tage of conciliation*
development. They steer away from *is its focus on*
forging agreements on specific issues *relationship.*
such as child custody and property
damage compensation.

Currently, the *systems* approach en-
joys tremendous popularity among conciliators. Family systems
theory states that one family member's problem stems from his
or her interaction with other family members. The problems rarely
result from deficiencies with-in the person. For example, parents
might view their son or daughter as a troublemaker and send the
child to therapy. The therapist generally wants to see all the family
members to see how they contribute to the child's behavior. Most
of the time, counselors trace the difficulty to destructive family
interaction patterns. Think about how family interaction patterns
affect your behavior. Perhaps you can identify some destructive
communication patterns that have a negative impact on you.

Advantages

The primary advantage of conciliation is its focus on relationship. People need lots of time to sort through their many complex
and long-lasting problems. Furthermore, the process remains quite
flexible and thus capable of molding to the specific needs of the
parties. The process demands a strong emotional commitment, but
the positive outcomes can outweigh this tremendous cost. What
value can we place on relational health? For very important relationships, the cost is almost priceless.

Disadvantages

Conciliation takes time. Therapy may last for several months
or even years due to the complexity of relational problems. The
costs associated with such long-term therapies can drain even the
wealthiest person. Not all therapies last a long time, but many do.

And they require a full commitment. Unfortunately, many people come to conciliation too late in their relational history so they cannot take full advantage of the process. They might use conciliation to punish the other party or to show someone else that they at least tried therapy.

Recommendations

Avoiding these disadvantages probably requires following two main recommendations. First, use conciliation when you don't really think you need it. Go to a religious leader or a trained counselor and ask that person to help you take stock of your relationship. Perhaps that person will notice destructive interaction patterns that you fail to see. Several of those patterns appear elsewhere in this book. This is the principle of routine maintenance. You do it on your car and your body, how about your relationship?

Second, don't deny that you have a problem. Denial is the most common excuse for not seeking help in forging a new relational definition. This denial leads to procrastination and the problem only intensifies. The sooner you seek conciliation, the easier restructuring your relationship becomes. Waiting makes dealing with problems much tougher. How many times have you heard divorcing couples say they tried therapy, "but we knew it wouldn't work." If you wait until you develop that attitude, you will doom the process to failure. Don't fail to give it a chance.

To find a good conciliator try to get a referral from someone you know, or through your place of work. If you don't know anyone to ask for a personal referral, look in the phone book for a licensed psychologist or social worker. Interview two or three people to find the person with whom you are most comfortable. Keep an open mind through the process and commit to the sessions. You might find the results amazing.

MEDIATOR

Goals

In most cases, mediators work very differently from conciliators. Instead of focusing only on relationships, mediators help parties develop solutions to specific problems. Typical problems include helping neighbors resolve conflicts and helping divorced parents create child custody and visitation agreements. Certainly, mediators try to deal with relational issues as they arise. However, mediators do not focus on relational issues exclusively. Mediators try to encourage parties to develop some kind of "working relationship" in which they can at least be cooperative enough to make a deal.

People apply the term *mediation* to a variety of different problem-solving contexts. In this book, it refers to a process in which the neutral third party helps couples make their own decisions. The couple controls the outcome and the mediator only facilitates that process. In some legal settings, mediators actually determine outcome. But as we shall see in the next section, that really constitutes arbitration and not mediation.

Structure

Mediation is more formal than conciliation. Mediators impose more rules on the process to aid in decision making. Mediators make the rules fairly flexible. However, they rely on rules to keep the discussion on track. For example, teachers train elementary-school children to mediate other children's playground disputes. In that process, the mediators begin with four rules:

1. Be as honest as you can.
2. No name calling.
3. No interruptions.
4. Agree to solve the problem.

In addition, mediators ask each party to tell his or her story and to generate potential solutions. Most mediators use rules and some kind of process to facilitate decision making. As a result, mediation tends to present parties with a more formal structure than conciliation.

Contexts

Mediation is perhaps the most rapidly growing dispute resolution process. It is quite common in the divorce and family areas to help divorcing couples work out child custody and visitation arrangements. Most of these programs work through the court system, and the mediators represent the court. However, in many instances, divorcing parties hire private mediators to work through a wide range of divorce issues. Community mediation centers also help people in many areas across North America. In these centers, volunteer mediators deal with tenant-landlord disputes, neighbor disputes, and business-customer disputes. Mediation is growing in the area of environmental disputes as well. Mediators address conflicts between government natural resources agencies and private landowners, for example. Mediators also work in a variety of educational settings to deal with disputes between school authorities and parents.

Strategies

As indicated above, mediators focus largely on the substantive problem that needs a specific agreement. To accomplish this goal, mediators walk parties through a series of phases. The phase structure offered by Kessler (1972) provides a general model for understanding phase development. She argues that mediators ought to pursue four phases. First, they should orient disputants to the process so they understand the rules, goals, and roles parties pursue during mediation. Second, the mediator gathers background information about the dispute to serve as an informational resource for developing solution options. Third, the mediator solicits key issues that need resolution in the dispute. One of the key issues might include the disputant's relationship, but the focus will remain on the primary problem that lead to the need for mediation. Fourth, mediators narrow the key issues into some specific proposals and select an option to complete the agreement. Research indicates that mediators who stick with this general pattern are more likely to secure agreements from parties (Donohue, 1991).

Some kinds of mediation, most notably in the labor context, often follow a different strategic course. In many labor disputes, the mediator meets individually with parties in a caucus session and helps them develop proposals on key issues. The mediator then takes these proposals to the other party for their reactions. Mediators return with counterproposals until parties reach an agreement. Foreign diplomats also use this labor model of mediation. Diplomats use this process when they find it politically difficult to meet face to face.

Whatever general strategy parties use, when mediation fails, it generally does so fairly early in the process. Many times, parties experience difficulty moving beyond the orientation phase or the first caucus session. Often this inability stems from severe relational stress, rendering parties incapable of using mediation. In these cases, they probably need a conciliator first to help build at least a working relationship. Donohue's (1991) research indicates that mediations failing to reach agreement focus almost exclusively on relational issues. Clearly, not all parties with specific problems are ready for mediation.

Advantages

Mediation's main advantage is that it works (Kressel, 1985). It works because parties take control of their own dispute. They generate the issues and the solutions thereby encouraging them to stick with the agreements they make. For example, most mediation programs experience between a 60% and 70% agreement rate immediately following the mediation sessions. Although agreements constitute only one criterion for success, these figures indicate that mediators generally help parties capable of being helped.

Cost is a second advantage of mediation. In one study (McIsaac, 1987), couples reported significantly fewer costs associated with divorce mediation than with the traditional legal system. Not only do mediators cost less than attorneys but disputes end more quickly than with other methods. Given its effectiveness and efficiency, more and more professionals turn to mediation as a dispute resolution alternative.

Disadvantages

Mediation cannot solve all disputant's problems. As indicated above, mediation fails to deal with severe relational disputes.

Conciliation addresses these problems. Some recently designed mediation programs (Girdner, 1990) try to deal with spouse abuse and other violent crime issues. However, these kinds of mediation sessions often look more like conciliation than mediation and require trained counselors to implement.

A second disadvantage deals with fairness. Criticism of mediation by Weitzman (1985) indicates that women suffer economically without lawyers. She argues that divorce leaves most women economically disadvantaged, placing them in a low-power position as they enter mediation. This low-power position forces women to agree to unfair or even abusive outcomes. Supporters counter this criticism by arguing that mediators try to steer parties toward fair arrangements. Research provides little evidence about whether or not mediators succeed in these efforts.

Recommendations

Think of mediation as a good alternative when you want to control the solution to a specific problem. If a problem needs both parties' cooperation to be solved, mediation provides the right forum, particularly if parties can work together. The trick is finding a competent mediator. The research cited above suggests that mediator quality contributes significantly to a couple's ability to evolve into a problem-solving discussion mode. Better mediators provide a forum that encourages problem solving and not abusive communication.

Above all, ask about the person's experience. How frequently do they mediate and what background credentials can they present? Can they provide references? Make sure you feel satisfied with the person's qualifications. Few states have laws about mediator credentials, so beware, and don't be afraid to ask about credentials.

Finally, you should automatically try mediation before going to court on just about any issue. For example, many renters fight with their landlords about housing problems. Should they go directly to court to resolve these problems? Mediation typically offers better solutions. It costs less, and it takes less time. Most communities offer experienced mediation services to deal with such matters. Consider mediation and look to your community mediation resources to help.

ARBITRATOR

Goals

In arbitration, the third party controls the outcome. Parties come before an arbitrator (or a board of people serving this role), tell their story, and ask for a specific outcome. The arbitrator asks some questions, and then decides the outcome. Arbitration seeks to provide expedient conflict resolution services. They ignore relational issues and do not permit direct negotiation between the disputants. In most cases, the law does not force parties to go along with the arbitrator's decision. They can decide to use the arbitrator as the final word if they want to do so.

Structure

Arbitration is extremely formal in most cases. The process requires a rigid rule structure. Parties take turns presenting their cases. The arbitrator asks questions after each presentation and then decides the outcome. The process is simple and direct. In general, arbitrators enjoy a fair amount of latitude with respect to what kinds of information each side can present. And the arbitrator can ask each side to present more information, if needed. The arbitrator can decide to meet the demand of either side or create some compromise settlement. Whatever settlement approach the arbitrator pursues is known in advance.

Contexts

Arbitration enjoys tremendous popularity in many contexts. Arbitrators mostly settle lawsuits of one form or another. A panel of three lawyers (not involved in the suits in any way) hears the case and then meets to decide the final outcome. These sessions do not typically bind either party to the outcome. Each can exercise the option of taking the case to court. However, arbitration laws carry certain financial incentives to discourage people from using the court option. People use this kind of panel arbitration to settle divorce disputes over property dissolution and other financial issues.

People also use arbitration in the labor context to deal with labor-management disputes related to wages, hours, and working conditions. Perhaps you know about some famous athlete who wants a particular salary, but the team offers a much lower one. In many cases, the parties call on an arbitrator to decide the case. Many consumer-based businesses also use arbitration to deal with customer disputes. For example, many car dealerships use arbitrators to resolve auto service disputes with customers. Universities also use arbitration to address faculty and student grievances. Check the arbitration resources in your area when you think this approach might work for you.

Strategies

Arbitrators use a fairly simple strategy. They listen to both sides of the story and then try to clarify each side's position. The key is knowing a great deal about the dispute to aid in asking the right questions. Developing a full understanding of the problem helps the arbitrators render a fair decision. For instance, a labor arbitrator must demonstrate extensive knowledge about labor law and the disputants' professions.

Based on this description, you can fairly assume that arbitration makes no claim about addressing relational issues. By selecting arbitration, the parties reject any further attempts to mediate their dispute. By not using a dispute forum capable of processing their relational concerns, the parties admit that their relationship is a second priority. Their first priority revolves around solving their problem immediately.

Advantages

The primary advantage to arbitration is its speed and efficiency in determining an outcome. Arbitrators gather facts and render a decision. This process works well when parties need a quick outcome, and when the parties care little about their long-term relationship. For example, most people place greater value on receiving fair treatment in a store than they place on developing a long-term relationship with the salesperson. Certainly the store wants good community relations to better serve customers. But salespeople and customers define their relationship quite narrowly around the single function of buying a product. As a result, arbitration works quite well in such narrowly defined contexts as buyer-seller disputes.

Disadvantages

The primary disadvantage of arbitration is probably overuse. In many circumstances, disputants turn first to arbitration as a way of dealing with their dispute. They ignore conciliation and mediation, even when their dispute would be better served by these more complex methods of resolution. Perhaps this reflects a desire to terminate the dispute artificially instead of really dealing with the underlying issues involved.

Parents often try arbitration first to resolve disputes between children. They impose solutions (share, take turns, etc.) instead of turning to mediation or teaching the children to negotiate. Children's disputes frequently focus on relational problems that ought to be confronted. Furthermore, children need practice at handling their own problems. Using arbitration as the only dispute resolution method robs them of this opportunity.

We carry this same overreliance on arbitration into our professional world. Many dispute programs emphasize arbitration when the relationship between the parties is critical. Employee grievances against administrators mostly use arbitration. Few companies provide mediation or conciliation services for their members. Yet, most employee disputes deal with important relational issues. Certainly, members rely heavily on long-term relationships for team-work in completing tasks. Most organizations would benefit tremendously by offering a full range of dispute options.

Recommendations

Based on this last comment, most disputants ought to use arbitration only after trying other dispute-resolution methods.

Negotiation, conciliation, and mediation try to preserve the relationship and perhaps even strengthen it. Arbitration avoids underlying problems. Turning to it first means that parties want to avoid these underlying issues. This same logic extends in the other directions, as well. Use arbitration before going to court, if you can. Instead of suing and using the court system, at least consider arbitration through your local community dispute center. Most communities offer such services, and they generally work very effectively.

ADJUDICATOR

Goals

Adjudication is really arbitration in the judicial, or legal, context. Most of the same principles apply to adjudication as apply to arbitration, but with some important exceptions. In particular, adjudicators want to secure a final, legally binding solution to a conflict. The parties may not want to go along with the solution; if they refuse, they violate the law.

Structure

Adjudication is the most formal dispute resolution process. Very specific rules and procedures govern how legal cases can proceed. For example, rules govern the kinds of evidence that parties can use and when they can use it. More rules govern who can serve as attorneys, and others deal with how parties bring conflicts before the court. In fact, the process is so formal and difficult to access that attorneys must manage this process. People need this structure, because the outcome is legally binding. The outcome is law. As a result, the process must remain unbiased. If everyone trusted everyone else to be fair, society would not need this kind of detailed structure. Unfortunately, parties come to court because they cannot trust each other. The structure serves as their protection.

In addition, the adjudication process is inherently adversarial. Each party forwards different interpretations and claims about the same problem. The court provides no neutral advocate for "the truth" or "what is best." The assumption is that one side or the other holds the truth. The side that tells the truth is the side whose case best stands up in court. For this reason, attorneys try to tear apart the other's case. Attorneys must know how to attack the other, defend against attacks, and bolster their own case. They must also negotiate skillfully if a settlement appears possible.

Contexts

Courts come in many varieties. A fairly standard structure for courts includes a district court that deals with traffic problems and other misdemeanors and a circuit court that is more regional in scope and handles a variety of serious issues like felony crimes, lawsuits, and marital dissolutions. Third is a probate court that handles the dissolution of personal wills, and nondivorce related child custody problems. Many cities and states create specialized courts to deal with other specific problems that might arise in those communities. For example, several states use family courts to deal with the full range of family problems. These courts handle runaway child problems, divorces, custody issues, and child support concerns.

When parties perceive they did not receive a fair trial, they can turn to appeals courts. These courts decide to uphold or to reject the judgments of district, circuit, or probate courts. The government also provides a federal court system to deal with problems that cross state borders. The entire court system is complex and requires extensive knowledge to navigate.

Strategies

The judge holds the responsibility of establishing a fair and speedy process for resolving disputes. Generally that means enforcing the rules and, when necessary, making a decision or ruling that is the most legally defensible. When a jury appears in a court case, it holds the position of adjudicator and makes the final decision.

Advantages

The primary advantage of adjudication is that it offers a final solution to a problem. It provides the basis of law and order in society. Without this kind of final option, society could not maintain law and order. Individuals would need to take the law into their own hands and administer justice.

This judicial process seems to work best in deciding issues of fact. Did the driver speed? Did the murder occur? Who is entitled to the money? The reason is traced back to the adversarial nature of the process. The process assumes that one of the two sides holds the truth, or is an advocate for the better way of handling the problem. Fairly concrete problems, like traffic violations, work best under this adversarial system. The court's job is to decide who holds the truth.

Disadvantages

What if a problem arises in this adversarial process for which neither side represents the truth or the better way of solving the problem? Consider child custody disputes in which each side wants custody of the child. Under the adversarial process, the court must award custody to one side or the other. Is that necessarily in the children's best interests? Studies show that joint custody, in which both parents hold legal responsibility for the child, works best for the child. Parents fight less when they both gain control of the child (Kressel, 1985). The adversarial system performs best when parties raise questions of fact but not necessarily questions of value. Quite simply, the best solution for all parties might not rest with one side or the other.

A second problem is the issue of forcing people to adopt a particular outcome. With both arbitration and adjudication, the third party decides the outcome. In each case, the slighted party might regard the outcome as unfair. This reaction decreases the slighted person's motivation to adhere to the outcome. In arbitration, both parties typically agree to abide by the outcome even though it might produce some grumbling for the slighted person. As a result, this motivation problem falls away with arbitration.

On the other hand, society forces parties into adjudication because they violated the law. As a result, parties often fail to abide by agreements dictated by the court. And they frequently reappear in court for the same problem. Child custody and visitation agreements forged exclusively by the court exhibit this problem. When parties have no voice in constructing the agreements, they feel less motivated to go along with them. For this reason, courts turn to other dispute-resolution processes, like conciliation and mediation, to deal with this problem.

Recommendations

People should use courts as society intends: as a last resort to deal with legal problems. When parties exhaust all other dispute alternatives, they should turn to the courts. Unfortunately, many people turn first to the courts, perhaps because they fear their enemies and need protection. Or they get mad and want to punish the other person legally. Many other ways exist to deal with problems. Try to find a different approach first.

Second, shop around for attorneys. Not all attorneys are alike. Find an attorney you can talk to and, above all, one that listens to you and hears your needs. When attorneys start forcing you to adopt a position that you know is wrong, then question that attorney extensively. Do not act passively toward your attorney. He or she is your advocate and needs to work with you like a partner. People that simply go along with what the attorney says may be doing themselves a disservice. The attorney may want something you do not want, and by remaining passive, you pay for that problem later. Being a good client also means learning as much as you can about your case. You might even read up on the law so you can ask your attorney good questions and work with him or her. The same logic holds true in getting your car fixed. People who know something about cars seem to get better service than people who know very little about cars. More informed clients simply get better service.

❑ Integrating the Dispute Modes

This chapter presents many important lessons about third-party intervention. Perhaps it is best to consolidate them.

(1) Third-Party Intervention Works Best When Parties Have Access to All Four Modes of Dispute Resolution. The best intervention programs offer all four options because they realize that different problems require different modes of conflict management. Conflicts do not always fit into one mode. Conciliation offers the best chance of addressing relational problems. Value and interest disputes often receive better treatment through mediation and arbitration.

(2) Conflict Management Seems to Work Best When People Start With the Most Informal and Least Structured Intervention Mode First. The less-formal kinds of interventions (conciliation and mediation) keep people talking to each other and let them try to work the problem through themselves. By the time they move to arbitration or adjudication, the solutions get out of their hands. The more informal modes keep the disputants involved and give control to the parties. They offer just a little help in negotiating. Trying these modes first may not only solve the problem, but parties might strengthen their relationships as a result. The opportunity part of conflict comes shining through when the parties work together to solve their problems. So keep the dispute process as informal as possible for as long as possible so people continue talking to each other.

(3) Begin Productive Conflict Management by Learning What Is Available in Your Community. Do you have conciliation or mediation services in your community? A little investigation might surprise you. As indicated above, most communities offer these services, but the centers often fail to publicize their services. You can find them easily in the phone book. Also most marriage counselors know about these services.

(4) Being Equipped to Address Conflict Also Means Becoming Better Informed About the Kind of Intervention You Select. Most people who go to court know little about the system. The same is true about conciliation and mediation. For example, conciliators come in all shapes and sizes. Some are social workers and look more comprehensively at the family. Others are psychologists and focus on the individual. Still others are psychiatrists who have a medical

background. The more you know about the people helping you, the better you can use their services. Shop around for the best professional and the best dispute program. Ask friends about their experiences. Remember, your goal is to find the best dispute mode and the best person to help with your specific problem.

(5) Conflict Management Works Best When You Think About Your Long-Term Relationship With the Other Party. Most people view conflict as a painful experience. So they either avoid the conflict or try to terminate it as quickly as possible. These two approaches obscure relational needs while magnifying individual needs. They also force us into thinking about our short-term needs and not our long-term needs. You already know that relationships are the key to personal growth. Without productive professional or personal relations, we experience trouble making it in life. Why pick an intervention mode that automatically sacrifices a relationship? That relationship might grow if you pick a dispute process that can examine it. So maintain a more long-term attitude about this important issue before you jump into any conflict intervention process.

(6) Productive Conflict Management Means Getting Help Sooner Rather Than Later. The longer you wait, the more relationally centered the conflict is likely to become. More time gives people more opportunity to violate personal needs. This problem happens frequently in divorce matters. Following a relationally troubled divorce, parties continue to escalate conflict. Sometimes parties allege sexual or physical child abuse just to pay back the other parent for past problems. These revenge motives build when parties ignore key relational differences. Avoidance is temporarily easier, but down the road, it exacts a heavy toll.

❑ Conclusions

This book is really about courage. Do you have the courage to confront personal conflicts? Can you stick with the confrontation once you initiate it? Can you risk relational growth from the conflict? This book helps you to strengthen your courage to step into conflict productively. Use this book to walk through conflict. It will hold your hand through the process. Remember, conflict can mean opportunity. Above all, when involved in conflict, control it. *Don't get stupid!*

8

Conflict Management Flowchart

Walking through conflict is a difficult task. Most people try to rush the process because they want the dispute over with as quickly as possible. The previous seven chapters talked you out of hurrying through conflict. The best strategy is to keep your cool and make intelligent decisions.

What are the intelligent decision points in processing a conflict? To summarize the book and give you an overview of the skills required to handle conflict successfully, this chapter provides you with a conflict management flowchart. Figure 8.1 outlines eight decisions and seven actions that walk you through conflict. The decisions are represented by rectangles and the actions are represented by circles. Each decision is a question that needs to be answered. Do not skip around in making these decisions. Try to follow the sequence shown here, because they direct you toward specific actions. If you skip decisions, you might take the wrong action.

Each action prescribes behaviors that are appropriate responses to your decisions. As with the behaviors, you will not need to take

155

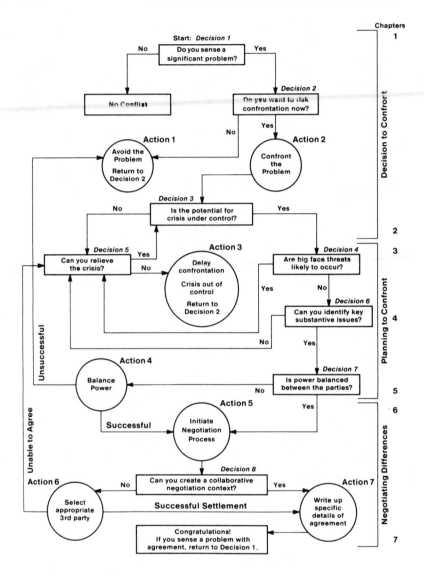

Figure 8.1. Conflict Management Flowchart

all the actions in the flowchart for any specific conflict. For example, in most cases you will not need to balance power between the parties. Or you might not need to delay the confrontation because of a potential for crisis. However, it is important not to bypass appropriate actions. If power remains imbalanced and you choose not to balance it, you risk an escalation to a crisis stage. So make sure you pursue the appropriate actions as you walk through the conflict.

As you look at the right side of the flow chart you will see that it divides conflict into three areas. First is the *decision to confront*. You can use Chapters 1 and 2 to help you make the first two decisions presented in Figure 8.1. If you decide to confront the conflict, Chapter 2 helps with specific strategies for addressing that need. Chapters 3, 4, and 5 assist in walking you through several important issues in *planning to confront* that conflict. Can you deal with the potential for crisis and face threats and imbalanced power? If so, you can begin the negotiation process. Once you decide to take this action, then a third set of decisions and actions are needed to help you with *negotiating differences*. Chapters 6 and 7 supply you with the appropriate negotiation skills and information about using a third party if negotiations break down.

You can use this flowchart in a number of ways. Use it as a general planning tool to decide if and how to handle some problem you are experiencing. Planning works effectively in dealing with conflict. Or you can use the flowchart to determine what went wrong in some conflict you recently experienced. Should you have paid more attention to face or power, for example? Should you have tried more diligently to pull out key substantive issues instead of simply letting emotional issues dominate the discussion? By correcting errors, you might be successful in allowing history to repeat itself.

The following sections detail the information you need to make the decisions and take the actions. Good luck in dealing with your conflict.

❏ The Decision to Confront

DECISION 1: DO YOU SENSE A SIGNIFICANT PROBLEM?

To decide if you have a significant problem, answer the following questions derived from Chapter 1:

1. Is the issue important to you personally?
2. Do you perceive that the other person wants something different from what you want with respect to the problem?
3. Do you think about the problem regularly?
4. Do you feel the problem threatens your personal needs to some extent?
5. Do you perceive that the other person will resist your attempts to discuss the problem or take it seriously?

If you responded positively to most of these questions, then you face a conflict that is at least at Level 2 (latent conflict) or higher. If so, consider confronting your problem with the other person by moving to Decision 2. This confrontation decision is complex, so try not to rush it. Consider your options carefully. On the other hand, if you responded negatively to most of these questions, then you probably have no conflict with the other person. Your conflict is at Level 1 (no conflict). The level of conflict changes as your answers to these five questions change.

DECISION 2: DO YOU WANT TO RISK
CONFRONTATION NOW?

As Chapter 2 indicates, this is a complex decision, because you really face two questions. First, is the conflict worthy of confrontation? Second, when should you confront the conflict? Let's take these decisions one at a time. To decide whether or not to confront the conflict, answer the following questions.

1. Do you want to preserve or strengthen the relationship with the other person?
2. Is the issue significant to you and worthy of confrontation?
3. Can you avoid becoming verbally aggressive during conflict?
4. Can you look for ways to use a collaborative conflict style in dealing with your problem?
5. Do you have enough time to deal with the problem?
6. Are you confident that your personal safety is not at risk in dealing with the problem?

If you responded positively to at least four of the six questions, then your conflict is a good candidate for confrontation. But you should also consider the timing problem. Consider the following questions about timing.

1. Are you ready to listen to the other's position?
2. Can both parties control their emotions well enough to listen to each other?
3. Is the situation free from distractions so you can discuss important issues?

ACTIONS 1 AND 2: AVOIDING
OR CONFRONTING THE CONFLICT

If you answered yes to most of the questions related to Decision 2, you seem ready to risk confrontation soon. You seem capable of controlling emotions and listening to each other. The issue and the relationship with the other person are important. You enjoy sufficient time to deal with the problem, you can pursue a collaborative course, and your personal safety is not at risk. However, by responding negatively to several of the questions, you demonstrate some hesitation about confronting the conflict. Perhaps the timing is not right. The situation may not provide for both parties' complete attention. The important point is to wait until you are ready to give the conflict your undivided attention.

❑ Planning to Confront

DECISION 3: IS THE POTENTIAL
FOR CRISIS UNDER CONTROL?

Now that you wish to control the conflict, consider whether you can control it or whether the confrontation will escalate into a crisis. To make this third decision, consider the following questions from the latter half of Chapter 2.

1. Can parties avoid threatening one another during the confrontation?
2. Can parties avoid challenging one another's personal needs?
3. Does the person know the confrontation is coming so it doesn't catch him or her by surprise?
4. Do parties have time to prepare their views of the situation?

DECISION 5: CAN YOU RELIEVE THE CRISIS?

If you answered negatively to one or more of the above questions, you need to think about relieving the potential for crisis once you start the confrontation. Be prepared to use at least the first three strategies of the Four R Method of deescalating conflict:

1. *Receive* the other's comments without interrupting and don't get defensive; allow the other to vent while listening attentively.
2. *Repeat* the person's comments as objectively as possible so you understand what the other person is saying; show respect for that person.
3. *Request* the other's proposed ways of dealing with the problem.
4. *Review* the options and decide on the best approach.

You can also avoid crises by making sure that you use rules when you confront conflict. Rules provide the structure needed to focus on the problem and away from personal needs.

ACTION 3: DELAY CONFRONTATION

If you feel unable to control the crisis, you must return to Decision 2. The situation may be sufficiently out of control and confronting the other person will do more harm than good. You'll know when you have failed to relieve the crisis when:

Parties engage in destructive conflict, as indicated in Chapter 1.
Parties use personalizing, complaining, sniping, or aggressing communication patterns.

DECISION 4: ARE BIG FACE THREATS LIKELY TO OCCUR?

Chapter 3 discusses theories about the role of attribution and face in conflict. The basic premise of the chapter is that making external attributions about the causes of the conflict, or threatening the other's face, can escalate the conflict to a crisis. To deal with these problems, consider the following questions:

1. Can you avoid attributing the conflict to the other's personality?
2. Can you see your own role in the conflict?
3. Can you avoid constantly attacking the other's face in the conflict?
4. Can you find opportunities to support the other's face in the conflict?

If you answered yes to these questions, you are probably ready to progress to the issue stage of the dispute and Decision 6. On the other hand, if you answered no to any of these questions, you may find yourself threatening the other's face. This threat to the other's personal need to be respected can escalate the conflict to the crisis phase. So if you responded negatively to any of these questions, you may find the conflict escalating to a crisis. If that is the case, return to Decision 5 and try to relieve the crisis using the Four R Method.

DECISION 6: CAN YOU IDENTIFY KEY
SUBSTANTIVE ISSUES?

Chapter 4 stresses the need to build structure into your conflict resolution attempts. Specifically, try to answer the following questions about building a structure to your conflict:

1. Can you begin the conflict by setting the stage for productive problem solving?
2. Can you separate the emotional and relational issues from the data, interest, and value issues?
3. Can you create multiple viable options for managing the conflict?
4. Are you patient enough to take your time in addressing the conflict?

I hope that you can respond positively to these questions. Positive responses move you to Decision 7 and the issue of power. Any negative response raises a flag about your ability to control the conflict and keep it from escalating to a crisis. If you cannot nail down the real essence of the dispute and structure the conflict process, then you may need to return to a crisis mentality and work to relieve the crisis.

DECISION 7: IS POWER BALANCED BETWEEN THE PARTIES?

Chapter 5 prepares negotiators to deal with the concept of power. Chapter 5 defines power as the ability to influence or control events and makes the point that negotiators must understand power in the context of their relationship. If power remains imbalanced in that relationship, then parties experience difficulty creating a collaborative negotiation context. To determine if power is balanced between the parties, answer the following questions.

1. Does each party have an equal ability and willingness to impact the other person's decisions?
2. Do both parties believe that they are not required to give in to the other?
3. Does each person realize that he or she cannot act independently?
4. Does each person understand the value of balanced power in negotiating collaboratively?
5. Are both parties about equal in their communication skills?
6. Do both parties feel personally safe in negotiating with each other?

If you answered positively to most of these questions then you can move to Action 5. You are ready to negotiate. However, if you responded negatively to two or more of these questions, then you might need to pursue Action 4. Let's take a look at each of these potential actions in detail.

ACTION 4: BALANCING POWER

If you believe that further power balancing is needed before beginning negotiation, where do you begin? Follow these general guidelines when trying to balance power.

1. Identify the nature of the power imbalance. Does anyone:
   (a) fear for his or her personal safety and thus remains reluctant to talk to the other person?

    (b) feel afraid to speak out for fear of retaliation?

    (c) feel inadequate in his or her communication skills?

    (d) feel unable or unwilling to influence the outcome of the negotiation?

2. Once you identify the specific kind of imbalance, work to restore that imbalance. Remember, the high-power person must take responsibility for this task. This person must see to it that the other can negotiate comfortably from a position of strength. The best way to do this is to bring up the issue as directly as possible. What would be required for both parties to feel comfortable negotiating? Identify specific requirements and try to deal with each one.

3. Check periodically to see that both parties feel comfortable with power levels. Power shifts quickly in negotiations. Checking on power levels helps people focus on substantive issues and away from their power concerns.

❏ Negotiating Differences

ACTION 5: INITIATE
THE NEGOTIATION PROCESS

Chapter 6 talks about specific negotiation strategies. If you think that the power is relatively equal among parties, then you can begin negotiating. When power starts to draw attention to itself as suggested above, it might be necessary to revisit Action 4. If power remains balanced, then move to Decision 8.

DECISION 8: CAN YOU CREATE
A COLLABORATIVE NEGOTIATION CONTEXT?

Your first decision in starting your negotiation is to decide what kind of negotiation you want to pursue: competitive or collaborative. Chapter 6 argues that in the long run a collaborative context works better for negotiators. Each side helps the other accomplish the goals. To determine how to create a collaborative context, address the following questions.

1. Are your substantive goals clear in your own mind?

2. Do you care about preserving the relationship between yourself and the other party?

3. Are you comfortable with your communication and negotiation skills?
4. Do you have plenty of time to negotiate?
5. Is negotiating with the other person the best way of resolving the dispute?

If you answered positively to all these questions, then you are committed to building a cooperative negotiation context. If you cannot answer positively to these questions, work on changing the problem area. For example, if time is limited, work to expand the time or at least be aware of its influence on the negotiations.

Now that you are committed to building a collaborative negotiation context, consider these questions when you actually start negotiating:

1. Can you negotiate face to face?
2. Can you freely exchange information with the other person?
3. Can you feel comfortable using softline, issue-based bargaining strategies?

If you responded positively to these questions, then you can begin to build a collaborative negotiation context. Remember the three rules for collaborative negotiation:

1. Be prepared to identify clearly the specific issues you want to resolve during the negotiations.
2. Remain firm about your goals but flexible about your methods.
3. Attack only the issues, not the other person.

If you feel compelled to pursue competitive negotiations, remember the seven rules for these kinds of negotiations:

1. Your opening bid should be just under the point of insulting the opponent.
2. Try to avoid giving the first opening bid.
3. Under most circumstances, avoid conceding first.
4. Try to keep your concessions fairly minimal.
5. Support your own position first, then worry about the other's position.

6. Make sure that the information you use to support your position is capable of persuading your opponent.

7. Don't threaten or attack your opponent; if you must, make sure you use it only as a last resort.

ACTION 6: SELECT AN APPROPRIATE THIRD PARTY

If you fail to build a collaborative negotiation context and further communication just escalates destructive conflict, look to a third party to help. Use the following guidelines to select your third party.

1. If you feel the need to resolve key relational differences, consider going to a conciliator for help.

2. If no divisive relational issues exist after the negotiation and you want the parties to control the outcome, ask a mediator to help.

3. If you feel uncomfortable with further negotiations and you simply want someone to make a decision for you, ask an arbitrator to help.

4. If you feel that a formal, legal decision is needed on the matter, and you have tried other third-party options first, ask an adjudicator to help.

If you reach an acceptable agreement using the appropriate third party, go to Action 7. If not, you probably have a crisis on your hand. Conflict has probably escalated out of control and requires a return to Decision 5. Let's assume that you successfully create an agreement and are ready for Action 7.

ACTION 7: WRITE UP THE SPECIFIC DETAILS OF THE AGREEMENT

Why do you need to make the agreement specific? The more specific the agreement, the less ambiguity there is to cause problems later. People must leave the negotiation table with a clear sense of what was decided. More clarity will make them happy.

However, if problems arise with the agreement, and they probably will, return to Decision 1 and work through the flowchart again. You might be tempted to take some shortcuts, but avoid this temptation. Remember that planning and preparation are the keys to effective conflict management. *Good luck with your conflict management.*

References

Donohue, W. A. (1991). *Communication, marital dispute and divorce mediation.* Hillsdale, NJ: Lawrence Erlbaum.

Felson, R. B. (1984). Patterns of aggressive social interaction. In A. Mummendy (Ed.), *Social psychology of aggression* (pp. 107-126). Berlin: Springer-Verlag.

Fiske, S. T., & Taylor, S. E. (1984). *Social cognition.* Reading, MA: Addison-Wesley.

Fitzpatrick, M. A. (1989). *Between husbands and wives.* Newbury Park, CA: Sage.

Folger, J., & Poole, M. S. (1984). *Working through conflict.* Glenview, IL: Scott, Foresman.

Girdner, L. (1990). Mediation triage: Screening for spouse abuse in divorce mediation. *Mediation Quarterly, 7,* 365-376.

Gottman, J. (1979). *Marital interaction.* New York: Academic Press.

Herek, G. M., Janis, I. L., & Huth, P. (1989). Decision making during international crises: Is quality of process related to outcome? *Journal of Conflict Resolution, 31,* 203-226.

Infante, D. A. (1987) Aggressiveness. In J. McCrosky & J. Daly (Eds.), *Personality and interpersonal communication* (pp. 157-192). Newbury Park, CA: Sage.

Janis, I. L. (1989). *Crucial decisions.* New York: Academic Press.

Kessler, S. (1972). Counselor as mediator. *Personnel and Guidance Journal, 58,* 94-106.

Kilmann, R. H., & Thomas, K. W. (1975). Interpersonal conflict-handling behavior as reflections of Jungian personality dimensions. *Psychological Reports, 37,* 971-980.

Kressel, K. (1985). *The process of divorce*. New York: Basic Books.

Leas, S., & Kittlaus, P. (1973). *Church fights*. Philadelphia: Westminster Press.

McIsaac, H. (1987). *Report of the advisory panel on the child oriented divorce act of 1987*. Special report submitted to Senator Alan Robbins.

Noller, P. (1988). Overview and implications. In P. Noller & M. A. Fitzpatrick (Eds.), *Perspectives on marital interaction*, (pp. 323-344). Clevdon: Multilingual Matters Ltd.

Ouchi, W. (1981). *Theory z*. Reading, PA: Addison-Wesley.

Pruitt, D. G. (1971). Indirect communication and the search for agreement in negotiation. *Journal of Applied Social Psychology, 1*, 205-239.

Pruitt, D. G. (1981). *Negotiation behavior*. New York: Academic Press.

Putnam, L. L., & Wilson, S. R. (1982). Communication strategies in organizational conflicts: Reliability and validity of a measurement scale. In M. Burgoon (Ed.), *Communication yearbook 6* (pp. 629-652). Beverly Hills, CA: Sage.

Rogan, R. G., Donohue, W. A., & Lyles, J. (1990). Gaining and exercising control in hostage negotiations using empathic perspective taking. *International Journal of Group Tensions, 20*, 77-90.

Roloff, M. E., & Jordan, J. (1991). The influence of effort, experience, and persistence on the elements of bargaining plans. *Communication Research, 18*, 306-332.

Sillars, A. L., Coletti, S. G., Parry, D., & Rogers, M. A. (1982). Coding verbal conflict tactics: Nonverbal and perceptual correlates of the "avoidance-distributive-integrative" distinction. *Human Communication Research, 9*, 83-95.

Sillars, A. A., & Wilmot, W. W. (1989). Marital communication across the life-span. In J. F. Nussbaum (Ed.), *Life-span communication: Normative issues* (pp. 225-253). Hillsdale, NJ: Lawrence Erlbaum.

Tjosvold, D., & Huston, T. L. (1978). Social face and resistance to compromise in bargaining. *Journal of Social Psychology, 104*, 75-68.

Walton, R. E., & McKersie, R. B. (1965). *A behavioral theory of labor negotiations: An analysis of a social interaction system*. New York: McGraw-Hill.

Weitzman, L. J. (1985). *The divorce revolution*. New York: The Free Press.

Wilson, S. R., & Putnam, L. L. (1990). Interaction goals in negotiation. In J. Anderson (Ed.), *Communication yearbook 13* (pp. 374-406). Newbury Park, CA: Sage.

Index

About the Authors

William A. Donohue is Professor of Communication at Michigan State University. He received his Ph.D. in communication from Ohio State University. He has published widely in the area of negotiation and mediation. His recent book *Communication, Marital Dispute, and Divorce Mediation* uses his model of interaction management to understand how couples reach, or fail to reach, agreement in the divorce-mediation context. Donohue's current research focuses on the crisis bargaining context and seeks to learn how police negotiators can better manage hostage negotiation situations. He teaches courses in conflict management and theory construction and is an active member of the Speech Communication Association and the International Association of Conflict Management.

Robert Kolt is President of Robert Kolt & Associates, Inc., a communications firm in Okemos, MI. His company provides a variety of communication services including policy development, research, public relations, and advertising, to organizations in both the public and private sectors. He has held several executive positions in state government and worked as a television news anchor and correspondent for several network affiliated stations in Michigan. He received his master's degree in communication at Michigan State University.